A Guide to Fathe

Seth Carp

Seth Carpenter, M. Ed.

Copyright © June 2018 Seth Carpenter

All rights reserved.

A Guide to Father-Son Book Clubs

To real men, to good men, brave and scared, wise and ignorant. To men who are willing to show their sons who they truly are, and to learn who their sons want to become. To men who cry when they are hurting, and ask for help when they can't do it alone. To men who speak out on behalf of women and men, and who are not afraid to say:
" I don't know. I don't understand.
I was wrong. I'm sorry."

Seth Carpenter, M.Ed.

"Anything that's human is mentionable, and anything that is mentionable can be more manageable. When we can talk about our feelings, they become less overwhelming, less upsetting, and less scary. The people we trust with that important talk can help us know that we are not alone." –Fred Rogers

"We've begun to raise daughters more like sons... but few have the courage to raise our sons more like our daughters." –Gloria Steinem

A Guide to Father-Son Book Clubs
Table of Contents

Introduction

When my oldest daughter was in 3rd grade, one of my wife's best friends invited her to join a mother-daughter book club, along with one other mom and daughter. In the beginning, they met once a month to discuss the book - focusing on a specific topic, common themes and individual perspectives, then chat. In a short time, they became a close knit group of caring, supporting confidants, who communicate constantly about anything and everything.

This blossoming has been transformative for my wife and daughter, who now talk about any subject that arises, the moment it arises. They have a line open on every topic - yes, even the uncomfortable ones - and nothing is sacred. For a parent of a child who is about to enter middle school, this is so much more than comforting. It's a connection that neither of us had with our parents as we entered those years when peer pressure commonly overtakes parental influence.

Lori Day's book, *Her Next Chapter*, written with insight from her daughter, has been instrumental in what my wife and her friends have accomplished along with their daughters. The book expertly details the process for forming and running a mother-daughter book club. Full of advice from their own book club experiences, along with book and movie suggestions and discussion questions (prompts, activities, and more), the book served as part inspiration, part model for this book.

Still, I had my work cut out for me, since there were/are plenty of vital issues to tackle – issues that focus on boys and their roles that needed in depth addressing, if I was to do this right. But, as you see, I opted against the luxuries of time and experience.

I decided to begin work on this book even before my son and I embarked on a journey similar to the one that had brought my wife and oldest daughter closer together. Then the #MeToo and Time's Up movements gave me added incentive to speed things up. Not long after that, the mass shooting happened at Marjory Stoneman Douglas High School in Parkland, Florida (just 6 miles from my wife's high school alma mater). This tragedy struck me with the urgency with which we need to address the way we bring up our boys.

It's crystal clear that we need to steer abruptly away from the tough-guy-who-doesn't-cry model. Instead of preparing them for adulthood, it reinforces a tired stereotype that is inaccurate, unhealthy and often dangerous. In referring to the extreme gender stereotyping that places strong, macho men directly opposite, weak subservient women, Justin Baldoni says:

"...this is wrong, this is toxic, and it has to end."

Mass shootings in the United States are committed by males. Boys are born just as vulnerable and impressionable as girls, and we desperately need to work on how we are raising them.

In Michael Ian Black's article from the New York Times, "The Boys Are Not All Right", he accurately points out that:

"...Too many boys are trapped in the same suffocating, outdated model of masculinity, where manhood is measured in strength...where manliness is about having power over others. ...and they don't even have the language to talk about how they feel ...because the language ...to discuss the full range of human emotion is still viewed as sensitive and feminine."

And, while this book is meant for dads to read (not sons), it's important to point out that adult male role models come in many forms. We know there are many different versions of Family. It may be a dad, an uncle, a (much older) brother or cousin, a grandfather, a long-time family friend, a close neighbor,...etc. It may even be a mom who is the one being there for the boy at this moment. For ease of writing, I use "father-son" throughout the book, but please know that this means YOU - whoever you may be. Honestly, the important thing here is that there is a caring, loving adult to go on the journey together with the boy.

This experience should be a pleasure, not a chore. Use what you need from the book to guide you one step at a time. You'll accomplish plenty by simply going ahead month by month, without being overwhelmed.

In this spirit, it's important to choose dads/adults for your book club with whom you share common values. This is not meant to be a debate forum. It has to be a safe space where members aren't expected to constantly defend their beliefs and where boys feel safe being honest. So take the time to assemble a cohesive group that is prepared to grow together.

I am a writer and an educator, but I'm also a performer. Working in the arts has placed me with people who regularly make and seek opportunities for self-expression. A regular diet of self expression is desperately needed for our kids as they constantly reexamine where they fit within the group. Those who are truly comfortable expressing themselves are far less likely to be among the perpetrators of violent crimes.

Of course, I can't represent all males, and this affects the scope of the book. I strongly encourage you to address the makeup and background of your group members and their specific issues. Our country and our world does not all look like me and my son. Dads of black boys, of Latinx boys,...of every wonderful, beautiful kind of boy - must have conversations with their sons that I cannot lead or perhaps even fully understand. This should embolden all role models to meet their sons where they are, and talk about those ethnically and culturally specific issues - especially the really tough ones. We can't shy away from the ugly truths, the stakes are simply too high.

Naturally, I will still bring up issues in my group that don't seem to affect me or my son directly. I will take care to listen to those who are experiencing it and follow their lead as best I can.

My son is still a few years from 3rd grade, so I'm actually still in the research and planning phase for our book club (my older daughter - who is about to enter middle school - is a veteran of the book club experience. She and my wife are supplying me with plenty of info and tips on what works and what keeps things fun and enriches the dialogue). While a future edition (editions) of this book will be forthcoming, I felt it was important to get this first one out as soon as possible.

Another bonus of this book club is that boys are in severe need of male reading role models (preschool and elementary teachers and librarians are overwhelmingly female). And when they do start reading, good things happen...

"When boys come to value reading, it also opens them up to new ways of thinking about the world and relating to others. That's because the daily reading habit broadens their understanding of themselves and people different from them, expanding their ideas of justice, fairness, and truth."
-Hillary Tubin, literacy educator

Meanwhile, my wife and daughter and their dear companions are still going strong with monthly meetings and highly anticipated get togethers. I expect they'll continue until the girls graduate from high school. Even then, I'm sure they'll wish they could carry on meeting and hashing things out. There's no age when it becomes desirable to close the book on book club.

Beginning with this book and our book club, I hope to embark on a similar journey with my son. Once we start the conversation, the door will be open to making connections and establishing a tradition of open communication for our sons. We can raise a wave of boys valued for their individuality, who recognize our shared humanity, brought up to embrace all their brothers and sisters as equals... and perhaps most importantly, embrace themselves.

GENDER STEREOTYPES

While I could stick this section on Gender Stereotypes in almost any chapter of the book, it's an important theme in ALL of them, and so it needs to be read first.

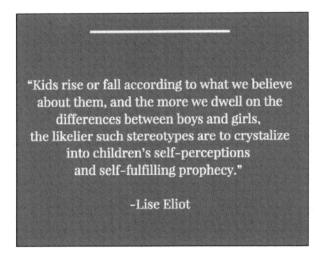

"Kids rise or fall according to what we believe
about them, and the more we dwell on the
differences between boys and girls,
the likelier such stereotypes are to crystalize
into children's self-perceptions
and self-fulfilling prophecy."

-Lise Eliot

It begins at home. Parents establish the stereotype before birth with the traditional barrage of pink or blue to tell the world exactly what's coming (as if any parent could actually predict what their child will be like). These colors were artificially ingrained into our culture by magazines, manufacturers and department stores.   There's no universal connection between gender and color. Yet most young children will insist that pink is a girl color and blue is a boy color. Society has taught them this, and - though it may seem harmless – it's not. It's a single line on a long list of things that children begin internalizing even before they can talk.

"Gender differences that exist become amplified by the two different cultures that boys and girls are immersed in from birth."
-Peggy Orenstein, *Cinderella Ate My Daughter*

Perhaps you've you seen the new gender reveal trend. The parents-to-be reveal... a glass of water. Why? Because gender is fluid. This may not be your style, but do yourself the favor of considering the implications of our sometimes vigorously strong over reactions to the gender alone of the unborn child. In other words, be incredibly happy about the baby. Jump for joy, scream and shout, fall to your knees and praise whomever you desire. But when it comes to the sex of the baby, maybe you could just say "That's nice."

Of course boys and girls are different. But let's not get caught up in stereotypes. Other than the obvious physical attributes, the differences are far less significant than the gender hounds want us to believe. Girls develop faster intellectually, so the relative immaturity of boys is mistaken for a difference in personality. Some motor skills develop faster in boys, so the relative lack of coordination of girls is mistaken for a difference in ability (or if a girl is more physically skilled than her female peers, she is ironically labeled a "tomboy"). These and other small differences are focused upon and reinforced over and over as our kids grow into young adults.

"Overall, boys and girls brains are remarkably alike... their brains appear to be less sexually differentiated than adult men's and women's."
–Lise Eliot, *Pink Brain, Blue Brain*

Even teachers are susceptible to this mythologically monstrous "boy-girl ability gap". They have it in the back of their minds (or the front) that boys are just better at some things than girls. For example, the fact that there are more male scientists and engineers would seem to back them up. Many careers are dominated by a single gender, and while there is crossover, it still sends a signal to the adults who keep track.

What many of these adults are not taking into account is the phenomenon of neuroplasticity. Bear with me, because this is the aspect of our brains upon which literally all learning is based.

Imagine a soft, warm lump of clay that is easily molded. The young brain changes more easily as it takes in new information.

"Every interaction, every activity strengthens some neural circuits at the expense of others... the younger the child the greater the effect."
–Peggy Orenstein

Our brains physically change in response to our own experience. This is neuroplasticity, and it lessens as we grow up. That lump of clay is harder and colder and less receptive to new information (we can learn, but it takes significantly more effort).

Accepting neuroplasticity helps us understand how our traits and tendencies are directly shaped by our experience. This also clarifies how nurture can become nature.

The fact that younger brains are more adaptable than older brains clarifies why:

"Nearly all of the evidence for sex differences in the brain comes from studies of adult men and women."
–Lise Eliot

Adult brains adapted to years and years of small messages teaching them over and over again to accept and adopt the stereotypes. Studies of children don't yield that many differences, because the differences don't exist.

My parents wanted me to be a doctor, but they would settle for an engineer. This made perfect sense to them, since I was good at math and science. They steered me in the logical direction. The fact that I read more than anyone in the family, and was constantly spouting verse and making observations about the world around me was largely inconsequential to them, for - other than being mildly entertaining - it was of no practical use. Parents often perceive connections they believe to be relevant to a child's future career based on a biased boy-girl world view. Gender stereotypes help to validate those connections.

Parents will even rely on those stereotypes to comfort themselves upon hearing that their child has misbehaved.

"...parents of boys,... find it easier to blame testosterone or brain maturation for every misbehavior and lagging achievement rather than examine their own nurturing, discipline, and expectations for diligence and self-control."
–Lise Eliot

For a fun (3 minute) comedic break, look up the "Let's Generalize About Men" music video from the show *Crazy Ex-Girlfriend*. It's a genius bit of what I wish were pure exaggeration.

There are so many subconscious stereotypes woven into the fabric of our daily interactions, that we need to be aware of - so we can start to change them. We tell a girl she looks good as if that's the top priority, when it should be an afterthought. We ask a boy a question about sports, or tell him he's good at something (usually physical). Let him be good at cooking or being creative! Consider the message in this girl's t-shirt, "Sorry boys, my daddy says I can't date 'til I'm 30." Fail. Or how about this onesie? - "Mommy's Little Hero." The mommy who gives birth is more hero than any child will be for a long time. If you're going to tell someone they do something "like a girl," either make it a compliment or bite your tongue. Girls can be fast, smart, strong, resilient, and fierce. Boys can get frightened and cry. Genetically speaking, it's our shared humanity - regardless of gender - that makes us such a capable team. If we haven't modeled this and communicated it to our kids consistently by the time they're 10, they could wind up being stuck inside the boy or girl box.

Kids believe gender stereotypes by age 10.

"We found children at a very early age—from the most conservative to the most liberal societies—quickly internalize this myth that girls are vulnerable and boys are strong and independent."
-Robert Blum, *Time Health*

The push of boys in specific directions, and girls in others is in practice at virtually all levels of education. Boys in preschool "like" to build things, while girls "like" to dress up. Boys get called on to answer math questions more often than girls, girls are expected to be more organized. These and a ton of other seemingly insignificant teacher practices combine to have a tremendous effect on what boys and girls feel good (and bad) at.

To exacerbate this problem, kids prefer to do things they feel they're good at, so they wind up spending more time on the stuff adults have steered them toward, increasing only those skills.

It's as if some minor difference in timing and attention are hijacked to create what eventually becomes this gigantic male-female gender gap. Even though it's little more than stereotypes, it winds up affecting test scores, career choices, relationships, and pretty much everything.

If we can at least **be aware** of these artificially manufactured "guidelines" for boys and girls, we can help to reopen possibilities for our kids. It's up to us to create the awareness among them. It's the first step to changing their thinking and broadening their learning.

At the same time, we can encourage teachers to ditch the stereotypes, and even un-teach them when they pop up. If we really get behind children and encourage them to be themselves, we can empower them to support each other and do the things they truly like - rather than spend their lives trying to "fit in," AND expecting the other gender to do the same. The bonus of self respect plus respect for the other gender is a powerful way to combat rape culture (See more about this concept in Chapter 7).

"...Although they live together and go to school together, boys' and girls' lives are very different, especially because one sex learns early in life to fear the other."
– Jackson Katz, *The Macho Paradox*

If your son is still a few years away from 3rd grade, here are several excellent picture books you can use at home to open discussion until you begin your book club:

- Jabari Jumps by Gaia Cornwall
- Too Shy For Show & Tell by Beth Bracken
- Those Shoes by Maribeth Boelts
- Hello Hello by Matthew Cordell
- When Sophie Gets Angry by Molly Bang
- Neither by Airlie Anderson
- The Invisible Boy by Trudy Ludwig
- I Am Jazz by Jessica Herthel & Jazz Jennings
- Last Stop on Market Street by Matt de la Pena
- Everyone Can Ride A Bicycle by Chris Raschka
- Not Every Princess by Jeffrey Bone & Lisa Bone
- The Book of Mistakes by Corinna Luyken
- The Boy Who Spoke to the Earth by Chris Burkard
- The Dot by Peter H. Reynolds
- Emmanuel's Dream by Laurie Ann Thompson
- The Invisible String by Patrice Karst
- Oliver Button is a Sissy by Tomie dePaola

~

I am confident this book offers the means to connect in a powerful way with our young boys, and is something our world desperately needs right now. If nothing else, we must open a dialogue with our children, as a way to keep them talking, and asking, and redefining who they are on their own terms. This is how it will stick.

Here is your action plan. Every month, from ages 8-18, you have this guide to make change. I hope other dads and caring adults will find this resource and run with it. Let this be part of our collective effort to raise our boys to show love, honesty, and compassion for all others.

1

How to Start
Your Book Club

If you do a search, you'll find a handful of articles about Father-Son Book Clubs. The majority of them seem to focus on "getting boys to read". While that is a worthwhile endeavor, it is not the primary goal I had in mind for my Father-Son Book Club.

In Lori Day's book, *Her Next Chapter*, she said of Mother-Daughter Book Clubs: *"Mother-daughter book clubs create a safe and empowering haven where girls can thrive during their toughest years."* This is the ideal. The focus isn't on literacy itself, but on using books as a tool for deeper connection and understanding between fathers/adults and sons.

In that spirit, I suggest finding other dads who hold values similar to yours when you go out in search of other father/son duos to join. While it could be useful to compose a group with different beliefs and ideas of what a boy/man should be, here we are doing the work of raising sons. This particular book club is not the proper venue for heated debate. You are aiming to create a safe space for boys to ask, explore, and share - so it's wise to put together a group of dads who are on the same page about what values they want to instill in their sons.

Because you are creating such a safe sacred space, it's important to keep the group rather small, around 3-4 father/son duos. On top of this, it's imperative to find dads with sons in the same grade. This is not about reading level, it's about eventually having a group of boys all entering adolescence at the same time and having a shared experience. Third grade or 8 years old seems like the ideal time to start the father-son book club. I taught 3rd grade for a number of years, and there is something very transitional about that specific age. They are still young enough to be silly and open(minded), but they are also beginning to to be critical and observant in a more rational way that will allow the conversation to be productive.

Starting in December gives you a few months at the beginning of the school year to find the right dads to partner with and make a plan. This way, the boys will be settled into their routine by then--starting up at the same time as the new school year might make it feel like one more thing on their plate.

I've made book suggestions in each chapter, but a great idea taken from my wife and daughter's Mother Daughter book Club is called The Book Throwdown (detailed a few pages ahead). Dads meet once a year (these moms do it in December) to narrow down a wide book selection that the sons will eventually vote on to read over the next 12 months. The dads should keep a group text going all year where they can share ideas. Sometimes a dad might text about an issue he wants to address, or some new behavior he is noticing. You can then research good books for that issue-- you'll be amazed at all of the online resources now to find the perfect book for the topic of your choice.

Throughout that first year of book club, keep notes- either on the group text, or have your own notebook (consider getting a composition book for every member) and jot down books you might want to read. When the annual meeting of the dads comes (go out for coffee, or grab lunch), you each bring 5-10 books to pitch for the next year. Together you'll talk about the things you want to focus on and then narrow it down to about 18 books. You'll bring those books to the next meeting.

Keep that group text or group email going so you don't lose track. Set up a consistent schedule and rotate houses and hosts. Let the other family members know that this is a special time just for book club and they will have to make themselves scarce.

Another fun thing I plan to adopt from my daughter's club is to note any specific foods they mention in that month's book, then bring that food to book club. Let father and son make that snack together (or just buy it – there's no need to be picky). Resist asking your partner to make it– although do NOT resist asking her/him for help if you'd like to learn how to make something they've previously mastered.

On that note, and in the spirit of being united, it's a considerate idea to find out any dietary restrictions of your club members and choose to bring only things everyone can eat.

A NOTE ABOUT RELUCTANT READERS:

Not being an avid reader shouldn't stop you from starting this book club. Whether it's you, your son (or both) who aren't big readers, let this book club be your own private librarian. You can even read the books together fifteen or twenty minutes a day. It shouldn't be a homework assignment, it can be a few minutes of bonding over reading each day.

When an issue pops up in your son's life, you can say things like, "Remember when Peter was upset in *Finding Mighty* about his brother? This situation reminds me of that because..." The book club provides an invaluable tool for bonding and growing, built slowly and steadily.

I recently saw Seth Meyers interview award-winning author Jason Reynolds who said he did not read a novel until he was 17 years old. When Seth asked why, Jason replied "...Because, to be candid, when I was growing up, what I wanted to see, what I needed to see-- the cultural details that would have directly connected themselves to my reality and my circumstances-- didn't exist in contemporary novels for young people. And because of that, I felt that perhaps books weren't being written for me." (I've suggested one of his books in Chapter 2 of this book and another in Chapter 3.)

It is important that you all, as part of a book club, feel you are reading stories that you not only feel connected to, but also that show you alternate perspectives.

AFTER THE FIRST YEAR

For the first year, I suggest you make plenty use of this book and the book recommendations and discussion questions in each chapter. This will give you a good foundation from which to take off on your own for the following years. **I've focused on male protagonists** in an effort to let boys see at least some of themselves in the books. As you move beyond your first year, I strongly suggest adding in books with other-gendered protagonists.

After a year of the dads leading the discussions and using questions in this book to lead them, the boys should be able to start leading sometime within the second year. One of them should write the questions to be asked at book club and facilitate the dialogue. Rotate through, and consider starting a blog where whoever leads the discussion can write a reflection on the discussion, or perhaps just start with a book review. This way you'll have a log of everything you've read, and a practical way to share it if you're so inclined.

THE BOOK THROWDOWN

The following method for choosing books was created by my daughter's book club a few years ago-- they call it The Book Throwdown (and it seems like a lot of fun).

The dads will bring the 18 books they decided on at their meeting. Each person in the book club gets 25 flat marbles/beads (so they don't roll away - you can find them in a craft or hobby store), or poker chips, etc. Lists are handed out with the 18 titles so you can take notes on the books as you go. Each book is pitched by the person who brought it (1 minute pitch maximum, USE A TIMER). Then lay the books all out in front of you, and everyone will... Vote by marbles, chips, or whatever.

There is one rule-- you cannot put more than 5 marbles on one book. Why? It can lead to books that only ONE person wants to read being selected. This way, you're truly choosing books that EVERYONE wants to read. The 10-11 books with the most marbles will be your books for the new year.
Next, assign the books to a month-- it can be random or you can go in order of most marbles to least, alphabetical, etc.

Again, The Book Throwdown is a plan for choosing books   *after* your first year of using the book suggestions in this book.

It's helpful to choose a consistent day for your book club meetings-- say, the second Tuesday of every month. You can always reschedule, but this way it's on everyone's calendar with plenty of warning. Doing it on a school night makes it a treat and adds a "grown-up" feeling to the whole endeavor. You can rotate homes, or pick a central meeting spot.

Here is one suggestion for the timeline of your monthly meeting:

Father Son Book Club 2nd Tuesday of every month
7pm Arrive & fill your plate with snacks
7:15pm Book discussion starts
8:15pm Sons go play/hang out and Dads talk/reflect/hang out
9pm Time to go home

A few good resources for choosing books:
www.Commonsensemedia.org
www.Goodreads.com

Common Sense Media is a great tool to use to decide if a book or movie is age appropriate. They have everything rated by age and explain why.

Goodreads is a great place to find new books.

Sometimes, the best books are found simply by searching online for exactly what you want. Just type in and search… "Best middle grades books on LGBTQ" or "Books for 9 year olds on social justice", you get the idea.

Here are some sample worksheets (modeled after the ones created by my wife) to help you get started-- you can copy them and use over and over:

Book Throwdown Titles for _____ (year)

Dads: Narrow down to 18 books total by Dec 1

Each book gets a 1 minute or under pitch... while listening, you can take notes so you'll remember which ones piqued your interest. Kids can get together and decide to throw out 1 book maximum before voting.

Only 10 books can win... which will be eliminated?

Books pitched by Father/Son Team #1_____

TITLE	Circle One	Notes
	Yes No Maybe	
	Yes No Maybe	
	Yes No Maybe	
	Yes No Maybe	
	Yes No Maybe	
	Yes No Maybe	

Books pitched by Father/Son Team #2_____

TITLE	Circle One	Notes
	Yes No Maybe	
	Yes No Maybe	
	Yes No Maybe	
	Yes No Maybe	
	Yes No Maybe	
	Yes No Maybe	

Books pitched by Father/Son Team #3_____

TITLE	Circle One	Notes
	Yes No Maybe	
	Yes No Maybe	
	Yes No Maybe	
	Yes No Maybe	
	Yes No Maybe	
	Yes No Maybe	

Book throwdown picks have been made!
Now-- cut out the months below, line them up on the table, and
assign each book to a month:

January	February
March	April
May	June
July	August
September	October
November	December

Tip: We take July off, and put the shortest book-- or a movie—in December

Tip: Take July off, and put the shortest book- or a movie- in December.

FSBC Book Schedule
for _____ (year)

MONTH	BOOK	WHOSE HOUSE?	NOTES
JANUARY			
FEBRUARY			
MARCH			
APRIL			
MAY			
JUNE			
JULY			
AUGUST			
SEPTEMBER			
OCTOBER			
NOVEMBER			
DECEMBER			

A NOTE ABOUT SPOILERS

This book is FULL of them. All books and movies I mention here or suggest for Father-Son Book Clubs are discussed in detail, which means I regularly include spoilers. This is your warning for any title in here. I can't in good faith equip you with tools to lead the discussion without addressing the themes and scenarios in these stories that deal with the issues we want to talk about with our boys.

2
Masculinity
(Boys will be... Human.)

"Children are born wild. And that's beautiful, it's wondrous, regardless of gender. Even when they're feral creatures, kids are reservoirs of tenderness and empathy. But some do turn into savages. And sadly most of those are boys. They're trained into it. Because of neglect or indulgence. "
-Tim Winton

It kills me to admit this, but I remember stomping on frogs when I visited my best friend, Peter, who had moved to New Hampshire in the last year of elementary school. Violent, insensitive, and just plain gross? - Yep. Inherently male behavior? - Nope. If you feel inclined to challenge me on this, I submit that such behavior should labeled as "immature" – not "masculine." Consider the fact that a baby girl would smush (or eat) an insect just as readily as a baby boy.

"I see masculinity as being how men behave at present. I think it needs to change to include behaviors that are at present regarded by many as feminine, behaviors that are sensible, life-enhancing and planet saving."
-Grayson Perry, The Descent of Man

"Boys will be boys" is the tip of the masculinity iceberg. The apparent innocence of this overused expression betrays the multitude of various regrettable traditions – formal and informal – that supposedly lead to manhood across the globe. This path begins early, as parents and other older guides choose colors, clothes, games, toys, pastimes and more for young males in their care. This trend of identifying things as masculine, or appropriate for men, gains momentum as boys get older. It's acceptance through societal silence and support (advertisements, casual comments, downright cheerleading) continues to give it strength. Some cultures involve more heightened traditions in which boys attain "manhood" only through extreme discomfort, intense humiliation, and even physical mutilation (tattooing, scarring, circumcision during puberty). These practices are alleged to symbolize what it means to be a man.

The basic concept is that men must be tough, and toughness is proven   through suffering without complaint. As a man, we are expected to feel pain (fear, anxiety, sadness,...etc.), yet not ever express those feelings. This cycle continues when the young participants grow up, then subject the next generation to the same systematic hazing, misinformation and cult-hood, which is NOT what it should mean to be a man.

My training for the US Army reinforced this expectation of toughness, as the primary method applied by drill sergeants was - "We'll just keep screaming at you until you get it right!" Don't get me wrong. The merciless repetition of combat and safety skills did actually prepare us to react automatically, once we were in battle mode. I'm just pointing out the relatively narrow acceptable range of normal human emotions built into our training as men. A man can get angry, confused, excited, disappointed, even inspired - but when it comes to any truly poignant or, god forbid, vulnerable emotion, that's a woman's domain.

The best I could do to battle that expectation during basic training was to make the other recruits laugh. I did so mainly by mocking our superiors. I was invariably punished for doing this, but not before the nearest drill sergeant watched in amusement for a few minutes before remembering he was expected to yell at me to drop and do push-ups.

While my capacity for comedy was building my upper body, I realized that humor was perhaps the only allowable form of self-expression from us men that wasn't particularly "manly." The ironic thing is that certain men disapprove of women who are funny - especially when they are funnier than those men.

This childlike stance of "You can't be like us and we can't be like you!" is the precise opposite of what we are striving to model for our sons. Let's be diligent in exposing this outdated version of masculinity. The one in which...

> *"Men are silent about these issues because other men keep them silent."* -Jackson Katz

Our boys will learn to be vocal as they experience us being vocal outside our comfort zone. Each uncomfortable truth we admit about men is a step back in the right direction for men.

Men are not naturally dominant over women, but this ideal has been pushed, learned and adopted by too many for too long (men are not physically stronger in order that they may physically subdue women. That is nothing more than an ugly thought).

> *"There is agreement among researchers... that boy's and men's violence against girls and women is not the expression of innate, biological impulses, but is the result of some combination of personal experience and social conditioning."*
> -Jackson Katz

It's bad enough that humans (mainly men) should "dominate" the earth with our shortsighted, selfish priorities. There's no evidence that it should be the natural order. Consider women's perennial roles as exceptional and loving leaders of family and education (to mention the tip of an iceberg).

In that spirit, please be reminded that **feminism is a call for equality. It is NOT an attack on masculinity**. This may bear repeating to our boys as well as our peers throughout our tenure as father-son book club members. As we repeat it, we will remind ourselves and our sons that...

"Strong, confident men respect women as their equals and do not feel the need to put them down or control them in order to feel good about themselves."
-Jackson Katz

I've quoted Jackson Katz often throughout this book as he has been pioneering this work on a new masculinity for over two decades.

It is all adults, male and female together who must foster new generations' abilities. Together we must praise their successes and provide support upon their failings. The younger generations must see men and women working together in order that they too may work together.

Working together doesn't mean we have to lose our identity. While masculinity is not under attack, we do need to work to redefine it. "Strong and confident" can go right alongside "sensitive and caring." A child needs to see the adults in his life expressing the same emotions as the ones he's feeling. As we lead our boys in the right direction, consider this: There is no trait that makes a good parent that does not also make a good leader.

Adults who regularly practice intimidation and violence make neither good parents nor good leaders. Intimidation and violence are not inherently masculine either. We need to role model masculinity in a way that allows our good choices to be viewed as powerful. And this modeling will be more powerful when it's witnessed by our boys when they are still young.

"Since domestic and sexual violence are largely learned behaviors, it is important to reach boys before they learn to abuse girls."
-Jackson Katz

It's easy and relatively weak to stomp your feet and slam the door (which is why children do it). But, it's difficult and powerful to show empathy, forgiveness, patience. We need to practice these traits in our dealings with children as well as with other adults. In this way, we can begin to dispose of terms like "toxic masculinity," that label maleness as inherently toxic.

Let's be honest, there is plenty of misogyny (hatred of and towards women) out there. While we can't identify and combat all of it, we can be aware of it and call it out when we see it. We can also teach our sons to recognize it and refuse to be part of it.

In her article, "The Feminist on Cellblock Y': This Prison Program Elicits Men To Study Feminism, & Question Toxic Masculinity", Maya J. Boddie writes about the documentary on "an inmate rehabilitation program centered around feminist literature".

"In order to counter that particular manifestation [of men coming out of prison worse than they went in], these men spend their days learning about the patriarchy, discovering the power of vulnerability, and personally combating toxic masculinity... Additionally, the program encourages the men to confront all of the areas where these toxic ideals of masculinity have prevailed in their lives."

We also need to ditch many of the dad stereotypes that serve to put us in an unfavorable light, while chalking our "inadequacies" up to being male. There are so many, and most of them infuriate me... The idea that dads can't do laundry, dishes – basically any of the indoor chores is just plain idiotic. If you can cut the lawn, you can use a vacuum cleaner (and vice versa). Anything directly related to the raising of the kids is generally considered to be mom "territory." You know that's BS too. If you can make a child, you can make their lunch... and breakfast and dinner. There is no evidence that females are genetically better equipped to raise children. Outside of the three B's (Bearing, Birthing, Breastfeeding), there is nothing a woman can do that a man can't do with equal effectiveness. Men are too often caught being lazy, so they themselves hide behind the stereotype that says they're just not good with that stuff. Again - pure BS.

Also, we are leading them towards being more nurturing, and away from bullying. Dads need to embrace this in conversation and beyond, because the boys will be constantly looking to us for modeling. Nurture culture is precisely what it sounds like, and it's the healthy direction to steer our kids in order to begin to dismantle the stronghold and insidious nature of rape culture. I'll talk more about Nurture Culture in Chapter 7.

We must conduct ourselves in a way that contradicts these stereotypes - AND call our sons out on them when they lean into them.

We're not just talking about the would-be jocks, bullies or other stereotypically "macho" boys...
Misogyny is so common that it is basically the norm among mass shooters (look up how many mass shooters either had a history of domestic violence or carried out the crime in retribution against a girl or woman).

Wait, there's more: NERD CULTURE is also rife with misogyny. Once again, it's not only the jocks, in fact it's highly misleading to stereotype misogyny in that way. I'll talk more about this in Chapter 7.

MASCULINE STUDIES? ACTUALLY... YES.

Dr. Michael Kimmel, founder of the Center for the Study of Men and Masculinities at Stony Brook University, asked students to list the qualities of a "good man", then of a "real man"... sadly the lists paint opposing pictures. We must address the fact that people commonly accept that a "real man" (tough, never cries, vengeful, apathetic) is not a "good man" (compassionate, fair, measured, tender). Dr. Kimmel says,
"the discussion of women's equality seems to be everywhere...with new attention being paid to the role men play in helping women achieve equality, and why it's good for them, too."

Why should this old-fashioned "real man" still occupy a place of respect in our society? Is he an acceptable role model for our sons? We're in desperate need of a shift in our philosophy of masculinity. Men dominate the statistics of bad news the world over. The way men inhabit their manhood has largely not been working to benefit boys - not to mention girls and women. Let us address this with our youth, now.

BOOK RECOMMENDATIONS
on the topic of Masculinity

3rd graders	**~Wilder Boys by Brandon Wallace** ~William's Doll by Charlotte Zolotow
6th graders	**~As Brave as You by Jason Reynolds** ~Holes by Louis Sachar ~Garvey's Choice by Nikki Grimes ~One Shadow on the Wall by Leah Henderson

Movies	• **Ferdinand (2017)** • The Last Jedi (2017) • Holes (2003) • Castle in the Sky (1986) English version

REMINDER:

Pre-read or skim the books to decide which ones will work best for your particular group and the current ages of the boys. While some of the books on the list for older kids might be okay for your group, some of the lower level books may also work well for an issue that an older group is grappling with. These suggestions are flexible - a jumping off point to get the dialogue started. I included issues that I strongly feel we must address, but the topics all overlap from one chapter to the next, since they share the same underlying themes.

QUESTIONS FOR WILDER BOYS:

- Do you think the way Bull treats the boys is healthy? Explain your answer.
- The boys' mom says to them, "We're lucky to have a man around here at all." Do you agree with her? What do you think she means by that?
- Do you think Jake reacted appropriately to finding a gun? What would you do?
- These boys go through a lot of hardship. Do they ever cry? When is it not okay to cry?
- What did you think of Jake apologizing to the bird before he killed it for food?
- Skeet taught the boys to sew as a survival skill. Some people would say sewing isn't for boys. What would you tell them?
- When the brothers get into a big fight about their mom, they don't seem to know how to share their feelings with each other except through anger . Do you think they could have resolved it better if they had opened up to each other?
- What qualities are important for a dad to have?

QUESTIONS FOR AS BRAVE AS YOU:

- Besides Genie, there are four main men/boys we meet in the book: Ernie, Dad, Grandpop, and Crab. How are they different? Do they

---

have different ideas of what "being a man" is?

- Grandpop says, "is it a girl's name if it's my name?" Are there such things as boy and girl names?
- Do you think it's a big brother's job to defend their younger sibling? Does that include beating up bullies?
- Genie asks, "Is who we are only based on what we do?"... what do you think?
- When their parents drop them off, there seems to be no mention of guns in Ernie and Genie's grandparents' house. Do you think they should have talked about safety before dropping them there?
- Why do you think Great-Grandpop killed himself?
- Grandma tells Genie not to mention the house or Great-Grandpop to Grandpop. Between Great-Grandpop, Grandpop, and Dad... how many of their problems could have been made a little better by talking to each other and sharing how they felt instead of holding it all in?
- Genie says he could never intentionally kill a bird and says "the fact that Crab could is totally freaky". Do you agree?
- Why did Crab try to force Ernie to say he was too scared to shoot a gun? Why do you think Grandpop decided shooting a gun made you a man?
- Ernie says, "I shouldn't have shot it, it didn't feel right." Have you ever been in a position where an adult pressured you do do something that didn't feel right (even if it was okay for someone else)?
- What do you think Ernie and Genie learned after a month of living with their

grandparents? What do you think their
grandparents learned?

QUESTIONS FOR FERDINAND:

- Valiente's father says to him, "You better bull
  up!" What does he mean? Is he a good father?
- Everyone expects Ferdinand to be a certain
  way just because he is a bull. Do you think
  that's fair? Why or why not? Do you know
  anyone who gets treated that way?
- Was there ever a time you felt you had to act a
  certain way to fit in? How did that make you
  feel?
- Ferdinand eventually gets the bulls to start
  sharing their feelings. How does that change
  their behavior?
- What did you learn from watching this movie?

3
Feelings
Part 1: Self

(Acknowledge them, Accept them)

When I was eight years old, my dad got a phone call that lasted less than a minute before he hung up and immediately went upstairs. I followed because I wanted to ask him something. I found him lying on his bed, which – for the middle of the day on a weekend – was unprecedented. I could tell from the doorway that he was crying, so I gave him his privacy. Downstairs, my mom told me that Granny (his mom) had passed away. I felt bad for my dad, and although I wasn't really upset (I was the second youngest of eight grandchildren, and hadn't enjoyed the benefit of a meaningful relationship with Granny), it made perfect sense to me that my dad was crying (that was his mom, after all). While I hadn't seen him cry often, he didn't echo common sentiment regarding boys and crying. And he certainly didn't forbid me from crying.

He was a pretty even-keeled guy, but I recall being aware that things got to him occasionally, and occasionally he showed it. This is something I suspect many of my friends missed out on.

> "Whether you are telling me not to have emotions or not to express them, either way you are wrong."

Everyone is born with the same range of emotions. While we don't all experience each emotion at the same level, we do feel each one. We should feel "allowed" to express our emotions as they arise. This is part of being alive and human. If you block certain emotions because you sense that you shouldn't show them you're not doing yourself any favors. A laugh or a cry is as normal as a sneeze, but we are often expected to stifle them. This lesson, taught over and over again, conditions us to behave as if we were robots (and I suspect predisposes many of us to require therapy when we're older).

Imagine regularly stopping yourself from sneezing, yawning, or – let's face it – going to the bathroom. This ridiculous practice has been widely accepted for generations. Children hear "You're too old to cry", but there's no age at which we stop feeling sadness. They're told "That's no reason to cry", and yet we know that our emotions aren't driven by reason. We feel what we feel – we don't think it.

Why are so many adult caregivers insistent on weaning us off of our emotions? "Boys don't cry." translates to "Boys don't show it when they are sad." This is meant to make boys and men appear strong. In reality, not showing our emotions makes people appear cold, uncaring, inhuman. There's nothing productive or helpful about these traits. A cold, uncaring, inhumane adult isn't likely to contribute positively to our society.

There's even evidence that it's quite unhealthy to bottle things up:

"...efforts to suppress emotions in order to achieve a goal have been linked not only to poorer memory but also to increased physiological stress and, over time, less satisfying social relationships." –David DeSteno

When my own children report to me that their teacher has said to them "don't cry", or "stop crying", or "there's nothing to cry about", or – I hate this one – "you're not a baby anymore", I want to march straight into their school and demand they explain to me exactly how the need to cry is a fantasy. Meanwhile the science (not new science, this stuff has been out there for years) to support crying is still right here.

In her article "Let the Child Cry: Tears Support Social Emotional Development", Diana Rivera explains some of the reasons why we cry: *"Tears serve as an important communication tool, allowing one to show his or her need for support... Tears are an exocrine process, and it's been suggested that they can relieve stress by expelling potentially harmful stress-induced chemicals from the body."*

We would do better to acknowledge their feelings as valid, and use that as a way to open a discussion. At the very least, don't dismiss their emotions out of hand, or belittle them. On the advice of Harvard psychologist Susan David, we should

Say to boys: "I can see that you're upset," or ask them, "What are you feeling?" or "What's going on for you right now?" There doesn't have to be any grand plan beyond this, she says. "Just show up for them. Get them talking. Show that you want to hear what they're saying."

ON PUBERTY

Sadly, many boys get their first information on sex and puberty from the internet. If you can establish your book club as a safe space where the boys can ask anything (and I mean anything) and get a truthful, respectful answer, you will have done them a huge service.

There are books out there that can help the discussion along. My advice as a parent (who still struggles to get it right after 11 years and 3 children) is to begin talking privately with your boys about these things while they are still of preschool age.

In the book club, the few months before entering middle school is a good time to discuss it as a group. One way to go at this is to find a good "puberty for boys" book-- I suggest *Boying Up* -- and discuss one chapter at a time tacked on to your monthly scheduled book. *Boying Up* gives a really good breakdown by chapter of changes occurring around this time. I like how she breaks it down by science (even the feelings) but then gives tools for talking about it and acknowledging the changes.

BEWARE FICTIONAL ROLE MODELS

There are some who hold up Star Wars (the first six movies) as a valid, specific example of boys (Anakin, Luke) being trained to suppress emotion. In the piece, "The Case Against The Jedi Order", they tell us

"Men's expression of grief is consistently demonized. Crying in particular is framed as evidence of a dangerous

loss of control. Whenever we see tears from Anakin, it's always meant to represent his weakness of character and communicate to the viewer that he's being seduced by the dark side."

Ignoring feelings isn't a sign of strength. It's stronger to admit your feelings. It takes courage to ask for help. The other (less masculine) option is to be afraid – afraid of what others will think.

I have been stoked to see the two new movies move away from this insidiously persistent stereotype. Rey is strong for her undisguised vulnerability despite her determination. In *The Last Jedi*, we see the exceptional power of women leaders and the dangerously flawed men who don't listen to them. *"Poe is presented as a character who needs to stop with the mansplaining and learn from the more seasoned female leaders in his life."* –Kayti Burt

Luke is the only reasonably healthy example of masculinity in this movie. His character even grows within the time frame of the film.

We need to retrain. We must re-allow one another to express our emotions. We have to encourage boys to acknowledge their sadness and pain, and support them as they reveal it. This will make a huge impact because it will help to reconnect people to one another. When we share feelings together, it's immensely more powerful than sharing words. If males can celebrate the joy of winning together – or watching their favorite team win – there is no reason men can't share loss, fear, and sadness. **And by the way, this doesn't mean you have to cut out your favorite movies or shows-- just talk about them in terms of where they fall realistically. Point out what you see and encourage an ongoing dialogue.**

Adults (usually men) have consistently attempted to thwart their young male charges' capacity for expressing any feelings other than those which fall within the narrow range of agreed upon "macho" emotions (anger, frustration, regret, jealousy, ...etc). They justify this as a means of showing bravery or strength.

"Men really do display less facial expression, cry less, and generally disguise their feelings more than women do. But this doesn't mean men aren't experiencing the same feelings."
–Lise Eliot

Again, strength doesn't come from hiding a part of oneself. Ignoring feelings or keeping them hidden from others is the least productive expression of fear. Ignoring things doesn't make them decrease or disappear.

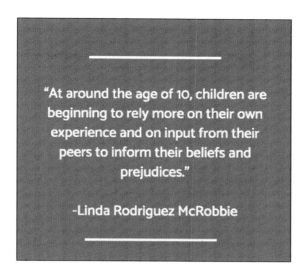

"At around the age of 10, children are beginning to rely more on their own experience and on input from their peers to inform their beliefs and prejudices."

-Linda Rodriguez McRobbie

We have an obligation to acknowledge our own feelings, and those of others. We must accept them as real and valid. We strengthen and grow as a society when we embrace our vulnerability. For it is our sensitivity, our innate capacity to feel, that allows us to act, based upon what feels good/right and what feels bad/wrong. It gives us the uncalculating, human ability to make decisions that lead to true progress for our communities and society as a whole.

BOOK RECOMMENDATIONS
on the topic of Feelings (Self)

3rd graders	~**Love That Dog by Sharon Creech** ~Tiger Rising by Kate DiCamillo

BONUS: 10-11 years old Non-fiction	**Boying Up by Mayim Bialik** Discuss a single chapter per month along with your regularly scheduled books. Aim to finish it the summer before they begin middle school.
6th graders	**~Then Again, Maybe I Won't by Judy Blume** ~Sunny by Jason Reynolds

Movies	• **Inside Out (2015)**

REMINDER:
Pre-read or skim the books to decide which ones will work best for your particular group and the current ages of the boys. While some of the books on the list for older kids might be okay for your group, some of the lower level books may also work well for an issue that an older group is grappling with. These suggestions are flexible – a jumping off point to get the dialogue started. I included issues that I strongly feel we must address, but the topics all overlap from one chapter to the next, since they share the same underlying themes.

QUESTIONS FOR LOVE THAT DOG:

• Jack says, "Boys don't write poetry. Girls do." Is that true? Have you ever written a poem?
• How did you like reading a book of free-verse

poetry?
- How was Jack feeling in the beginning of the book compared to how he felt at the end?
- Do you think writing the poems helped Jack feel better? Why or why not?
- Did Walter Dean Myers coming to Jack's school change anything for Jack? How?
- What do you do when you are sad? Do you wish you had more ideas for what to do when you're sad or mad to make you feel better?

QUESTIONS FOR THEN AGAIN, MAYBE I WON'T:

- On the drive away from the old house to their new house, Tony is very sad. He said, "I don't cry anymore. I'm too old for that baby stuff..." and he locked himself in the bathroom to cry quietly. Why does he think only babies cry? Have you ever seen an adult cry?
- After he isn't treated kindly by the 9th grade cashiers, Tony says, "Next year I plan to treat the new 7th graders the same way." What do you think of that?
- Tony worries a lot about changes happening in his body. He worries so much he sometimes gets stomach aches. What do you do if you're that worried about something? What do you think Tony should do?
- Tony worries when he notices Joel stealing things. What should he have done? What would you have done?
- Do you think Tony should have watched Lisa getting changed in her window? What do you do when something you *really* want to do is not the right thing to do?
- Tony's dad tries to talk to him about sex, but

doesn't end up saying too much. Do you think it was a helpful talk for Tony?

- Were you surprised when Joel offered the boys beer?
- Tony gets upset by everyone in his family suddenly caring so much about money. He says, "Maybe kids don't always want you to give them everything." What do kids want?
- Do you think Tony and his parents have a good relationship? Why or why not?

QUESTIONS FOR INSIDE OUT:

- Why doesn't Riley tell her parents how she is feeling? Have you ever felt like you had to be happy for someone else when you felt sad?
- Have you ever cried at school? What did you think of how everyone in the class reacted (or didn't react) to Riley crying?
- We find out Sadness is very important because she lets people know that Riley needs help. Is it possible to be joyful all the time? What did you learn about the (real) emotions of sadness and joy?
- Why did Riley think running away would help? Do you think running away is a good idea? What would you do if you were in her position?
- Do you feel like you can be honest with your parents about how you are feeling?
- If you had Emotion Characters in your head, what would they be like? What would your "personality islands" be like?

4
Feelings
Part 2: Relationships

(There are other people here, too.)

Raking leaves was one of my favorite chores growing up. But every time I headed out to the yard, my mom would only have to wait about 5 minutes before looking out the window to find me leaning on the rake in a sea of leaves, staring off into space. She'd call my name and I'd get back to work. She regularly introduced me as her "little daydreamer." She was right, but more specifically, I was a loner. It's not that I didn't like company, it's just that I found it far easier to commune with myself than to relate to other people.

I wasn't anti-social. But I was aware of the struggle to connect effectively with others - even in simple conversation. Listening takes a back seat, because we are absorbed in our own perspective. Good relationships happen when we listen and take the next step of actually giving a damn.

If you're feeling particularly good - or bad, you might need to be yanked out of your perspective long enough to look into someone else's eyes and notice that someone else feels a whole lot different than you do. But if your mom isn't around to lean out the window and call your name, you're on your own to wake up.

Since we are generally inclined to value our own perspective over that of others, it can be tempting to dismiss them along with their perspectives. We men must STOP DOING THIS. It's rude, as well as a dangerous aspect of misplaced masculinity. People think men don't listen with women in mind, because we often don't. It's become far too common in our society. It's reflected regularly in our politics and our headlines. In social forums, this prioritizing of one's own perspective over another's contributes significantly to rape culture. Some still promote the idea that men need to rescue women or protect them. In addition to being outdated, this has never been truly accurate. What's more it can lead to treating women as if they are children, which is condescending, to say the least.

This is why poor relationship skills in young ones should be red flags. We need to teach our sons that you can be selfish at times, but you still need to listen to the needs and wants of others. We need to steer them towards nurture culture (the opposite of rape culture) while they are young. In order for this to happen, they will need opportunities to listen.

Boys and girls aren't born with different tendencies in terms of how they handle relationships. They learn those differing tendencies again and again and again while growing up. Why so much repetition? People will leap at the chance to point out differences between the sexes.

"Focusing on extremes leads to stereotypes... so anytime people see a difference, especially one as emotionally significant as sex (gender), we tend to exaggerate it."
–Lise Eliot

I surveyed dads about valuable lessons they learned from their fathers, and what was important for them to instill in their own sons. The majority of answers (slightly more than half) skewed toward taking care of oneself (i.e. "You can be anything you want to be", "Believe in yourself", "Always do your best"), as opposed to improving the world around them (i.e. "Be kind to others."). A balance of both is best, to be sure. But ultimately, we have to embrace our humanity, which in large part involves being collaborative members of society. Loners or not, our boys should be able to feel connected to other kids growing up, especially when they hear or read their stories.

I also surveyed the dads to ask what they wish they had from their dads growing up. It's no surprise that by far the most common answer was some version of "more time".

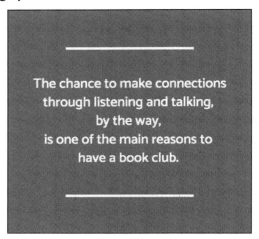

The chance to make connections through listening and talking, by the way, is one of the main reasons to have a book club. It's a scheduled time to get together with our sons and model for them, how to relate. We want them to really feel like talking and listening with no expectations or judgement.

In his Ted Talk "Expanding Masculinity: Moving Beyond Boys Will Be Boys", Blake Spence says "If we try our best not to judge others, it allows other people to feel safe in our presence. When we feel safe, we relax, we open up-- it's where great friendships and relationships start."

In the video "Boys and Respectful Relationships", Dr. Justin Coulson talks about how boys learn from a very early age to push down their emotions (I really hope you check this out, it's only 6 minutes).

The more I read and watch and listen, the more clear it becomes how father-son book clubs can be a huge part of the antidote to so many issues our boys are facing.

When our sons see and hear us listening without judging, and being honest and open about our own experiences, they will have the green light to do the same.

This won't necessarily be easy for me, as a loner, who has often kept my thoughts and feelings ...to myself. Honestly, I rarely talk about myself, my concerns or issues – even to family and close friends. My wife has to regularly remind me to share my stories with my kids or tell them how I have felt about things. I consider myself fairly evolved, very progressive. But this is part of an overly inflated self-image (which is a fancy way of saying that I'm being dishonest with myself). The most disturbing example that comes to mind is my reaction to my mom's passing. When I got the news that my mother had died, no tears came... – not right away, nor later that day or night, nor in the following week. I had plenty opportunity to drop my guard and feel and show the loss. But I never did.

I think most of us have to practice being more open and vulnerable. I want to make sure that my son learns to share the kinds of things that I didn't share while growing up, and even now am not inclined to bring out to people - even those who I know will listen without judgement.

Book Club gives us a wonderful forum, a safe place to begin talking about these things. We can ask about the characters and how they felt- it's a convenient bridge to get to feeling comfortable talking about ourselves, and teaching our sons to make it a habit. And, it's very likely that in the process, they will have plenty to teach us as well.

Imagine the healing possibilities of a support group, just for growing up. You know our boys need this outlet. It's so healthy and stress-relieving. And we know too many boys have resorted to unhealthy and sometimes unspeakable measures to express themselves. We can largely assume they didn't have the benefit of being part of a book club.

Good movies, with relatable role models, can also help keep the conversation going.

"...films can help kids cope better when life's struggles hit them for real. They've already experienced some of the associated emotions vicariously. They've seen how the characters handle the situation. Perhaps they've even thought about what they'd do in the same position. If modern kids' films can help the next generation grow into resilient, self-aware, inclusive adults, I say: keep them coming."
-Lucinda Everett

BOOK RECOMMENDATIONS
on the topic of Feelings (Relationships)

3rd graders	**~Wild Wings by Gill Lewis** ~The Magic Misfits by Neil Patrick Harris
6th graders	**~Posted by John David Anderson** ~Finding Mighty by Sheela Chari

Movies	<ul><li>**Coco (2017)**</li><li>Whisper of the Heart (1995) English version</li><li>Ronja, The Robber's Daughter (Studio Ghibli series, 2014-15)</li></ul>

REMINDER:

Pre-read or skim the books to decide which ones will work best for your particular group and the current ages of the boys. While some of the books on the list for older kids might be okay for your group, some of the lower level books may also work well for an issue that an older group is grappling with. These suggestions are flexible – a jumping off point to get the dialogue started. I included issues that I strongly feel we must address, but the topics all overlap from one chapter to the next, since they share the same underlying themes.

QUESTIONS FOR WILD WINGS:

- Iona says, "People are like rivers. You've got to learn to look beneath the surface, to see what lies deeper in." How do you do that?
- Callum's friends said unkind things about Iona. Why do you think he agreed with them? What do you think you would do?
- Describe the difference between Callum's friendship with Rob & Euan and his friendship with Iona.
- At a certain point, Callum can't stand listening to Rob talk badly about Iona and punches him in the face. Why do you think he resorts to punching him instead of talking/yelling back?
- When Callum tells Rob & Euan about how he and Iona saved Iris-- Rob makes fun of the name which causes Cal to say, "Why d'you have to make a stupid, bloody joke out of everything?" Why do you think he got so mad

at Rob?
- What do you think of how Jeneba's village worked together to help find Iris? How did that inspire Cal and his town?
- There are so many different relationships in this book to think about: friendship, parents, siblings, adult friends (like Hamish), your town or village. What did you learn about relationships from this book?

QUESTIONS FOR POSTED:

- Frost says, "I found the people that weren't quite like other people, and we used that difference as glue." What does he mean? What does his mom mean by "find your people and make your tribe"?
- Why do you think Wolf invited Rose to sit with them at lunch? Her arrival shakes up their foursome a bit-- how does it change each person at first?
- In this book, the kids seem to do a lot of stuff without any adults noticing. Is that realistic?
- Do you think the Post-It notes get just as bad as the kids saying mean things over the internet? Worse? Better? Explain.
- Wolf shares things with Rose he never brought up with the guys. Why?
- After Rose wins the Gauntlet run, what did you think of what she chose to write on the Post-It she had Cameron wear?
- How do you know someone is a good friend?

QUESTIONS FOR COCO:

- Miguel's family puts pictures of all their ancestors on the ofrenda to remember them. Do you have a way to remember your ancestors in your family? Can you name your great-grandparents or great-aunts or uncles?
- Miguel feels torn between his dreams of playing music and being loyal to his family. Do you think his family is easy to talk to about this conflict inside him?
- There are a lot of dead people in Coco, but they feel just as real as the living characters. Did this movie make you feel more afraid of death, or more comfortable?
- When Miguel meets Hector's friend who fades away we learn that people are only kept "alive" in the afterlife by people remembering them. Did this make you want to learn more about your ancestors and remember them? Are you curious about all of your relatives you didn't get a chance to meet?
- Did this movie change how you feel about death?
- When Miguel tries to play the song for Coco, Abuelita tries to stop him-- but his father sees him crying and stops her and allows him to play. Why do you think his father seeing him cry helped?
- What was Miguel able to achieve for his family at the end? Do you think he helped just Hector-- or Coco and everyone else in the family?

5
Empathy

"..empathy is the kindling that fires compassion in our hearts, impelling us to help others in distress."
-Yudhijit Bhattacharjee

While hiking as a kid, on one of our many family trips into the New England wilderness, I lagged behind in the cold rain on the summit of a mountain because there were two trails leading down. I was afraid someone was going to choose the wrong trail. I lingered so long that hypothermia began to set in. It was a pretty dumb thing to do with no rain gear, but it came from a place of natural concern.

Empathy is defined as *an intrinsic ability of the brain to experience how another person is feeling.* Researchers have discovered that most people are born with this ability ("The Science of Good and Evil", Yudhijit Bhattacharjee, *National Geographic*). It's even been observed in babies younger than six months.

Our brains actually have a whole series of components that are active when we empathize with others.

Not surprisingly, all brains aren't created equal. Scientists have "measured" the empathy in individuals by asking questions meant to elicit concern for the well-being of others. They discovered a wide range of people, with "extreme altruists" on one end and psychopaths (most psychopaths are men) on the other. The bulk of humanity rests somewhere in the middle of that spectrum. They also found that the degree of hard-wired empathy in individuals can actually grow depending on a number of things, including how they are raised.

A nurturing environment can go a very long way. Parents, peers, and role models who nurture and reward good behavior can systematically increase empathetic responses in their children/charges.

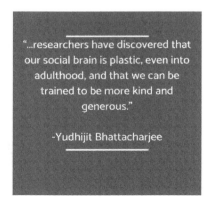

"...researchers have discovered that our social brain is plastic, even into adulthood, and that we can be trained to be more kind and generous."

-Yudhijit Bhattacharjee

Tania Singer, a neuroscientist Bhattacharjee interviews in his piece, used empathy and compassion together to train subjects to direct warmth and kindness toward those around them. This positive feeling tended to be contagious as it compounded into an "ever widening circle of love." Singer has recommended compassion training in schools.

Reading itself is actually a very effective way to promote and reinforce empathy. In her article in Scientific American, Julianne Chiaet documents how reading literary fiction actually increased students' *"...capacity to understand what others are thinking and feeling."*

> *"We know that reading builds empathy. Research has suggested that Harry Potter readers are strongly empathetic. NPR's podcast Rough Translation featured a man who found empathy and sanity in Anna Karenina. There is a reason Nazis fear books; empathy can defang hate."*
> –Julianne Chiaet

We should all be in the habit of accessing our own empathy within ourselves, and modeling it for our children. And we need to expect if from them regularly. The more we notice when something's bothering them, the more likely they'll notice when someone else is upset. Sometimes the only message we have to interpret is body language, and we owe it to them to be receptive, or they'll think we don't care.

"If we don't recognize... the challenges they're facing... they won't see us as a resource." - Rosalind Wiseman

Sometimes it's tempting to work against empathy, because we want those who come after us to suffer like we did. It's all too common, and somewhat understandable to fall into the - "I had to go through that, so they do too" mindset. Let's accept that many of us have exhibited blind obedience, tolerated mistreatment and endured some level of similar crap during childhood. There's no reason to tell kids they have to suffer just because we did. We find a way to make things better that includes respect, self-control and responsibility. Above all we work to keep the lines of communication open - even when it seems like a constant struggle.

> After all, there's no more accurate description of parenting, than a constant struggle.

RACISM

Many non-POCs (persons of color) raised in progressive households were taught to "not see color". We know in 2018 this is ridiculous- of course we see color. The biggest mistake parents can make on race is to make it a taboo topic and pretend everyone is treated equally. It is essential that we teach our children to acknowledge race and racism and stand in the truth of it.

In her 2014 blog post that was so popular she wrote a book on it (*Why I'm No Longer Talking to White People about Race*, 2017) Reni Eddo-Lodge said, *"Amidst every conversation about Nice White People feeling silenced by conversations about race, there is a sort of ironic and glaring lack of understanding or empathy for those of us who have been visibly marked out as different for our entire lives, and live the consequences. It's truly a lifetime of self-censorship that people of colour have to live. The options are: speak your truth and face the reprisal, or bite your tongue and get ahead in life. It must be a strange life, always having permission to speak and feeling indignant when you're finally asked to listen. It stems from white people's never questioned entitlement, I suppose."*

Ta-Nehisi Coates says in *Between the World and Me* (written as a letter to his son), "I was a curious boy, but the schools were not concerned with curiosity. They were concerned with compliance... When our elders presented school to us, they did not present it as a place of high learning but as a means of escape from death and penal warehousing." We must acknowledge that school can be a very different place for each student, and race can be a big part of the why.

If you want to dig deeper, read Mychal Denzel Smith's *Invisible Man, Got the Whole World Watching: A Young Black Man's Education.* Or even just watch his interview with Trevor Noah. Look up the suggested video below ("A Conversation About Growing up Black") and watch it with your son. (Your 8-year-old may not understand it all, but it is appropriate, and only 5 minutes long).

I have chosen several books over these chapters that depict characters of different races, backgrounds, and faiths. I hope that reading about these characters will spark healthy, meaningful discussion on race and culture in your book club.

ON LISTENING TO WOMEN

It's essential that we don't miss opportunities to teach boys the importance of listening to girls and women. We must teach them to listen to their experience, because in the past, the need to value women as equals has been decidedly not self-evident. We must truly take in and honor their perspective.

When they tell you their experience, don't tell them they're mistaken or wrong. Don't tell them what they should do, or what they should have done.

We, as men, cannot fully grasp that - with almost every move a girl or woman makes - she's calculating the risk of being harassed or assaulted.

> *"Time's up on women being held responsible for men's bad behavior. It's men's responsibility to change men's bad behavior."*
> –Tracee Ellis Ross

Children have long been first in line to be shushed (perhaps just a tad ahead of women). It's a habit we need to shed, as we sit and talk, and listen to our sons. Through this open-minded, open-hearted listening, we'll hear the sounds that others have worked - at times intentionally, at times subconsciously - to drown out.

BOOK RECOMMENDATIONS
on the topic of Empathy

3rd graders	~**The One and Only Ivan** by Katherine Applegate ~Wonder by R.J. Palacio ~Freak the Mighty by Rodman Philbrick
6th graders	~**The Watsons Go to Birmingham** by Christopher Paul Curtis ~Alan & Naomi by Myron Levoy

Movies/ TV	• **Ponyo** (2008) English version • Alan & Naomi (1992) • E.T. (1982) • The Watsons Go to Birmingham (2013) • A Conversation About Growing up Black by Joe Brewster and Perri Peltz (2015)

REMINDER:

Pre-read or skim the books to decide which ones will work best for your particular group and the current ages of the boys. While some of the books on the list for older kids might be okay for your group, some of the lower level books may also work well for an issue that an older group is grappling with. These suggestions are flexible – a jumping off point to get the dialogue started. I included issues that I strongly feel we must address, but the topics all overlap from one chapter to the next, since they share the same underlying themes.

QUESTIONS FOR THE ONE AND ONLY IVAN:

- Ivan recalls some of his past, but does he miss the jungle? Why or why not?
- Describe the friendship between Julia and Ivan? What are their connections?
- If Bob is so independent, why does he visit Ivan and the other animals so often?
- How does Ruby change Ivan's perspective? How does Ivan respond to Stella's death?
- Why does George put Ivan's painting up on the billboard when he knows Mack might fire him?
- Mack says "Thanks for nothing, George...". Do you think Mack still feels the same way after all of the animals have been moved?
- Does Ivan ever become a true silverback? At what point? Why do you think so?

QUESTIONS FOR THE WATSONS GO TO BIRMINGHAM:

- Kenny calls Byron's tears "big juicy crybaby tears". What does he mean by that?
- The bus driver defends Rufus and his brother to the other kids. Why do you think he did that when he's never stepped in to defend anyone else before?
- Rufus said, "I didn't think you was like all

them other people." Why could Rufus tolerate that reaction from other kids but not Kenny?

- Kenny notices that Byron feels awful after killing that bird, but he never feels bad after torturing kids. Why do you think that is?
- Do the brothers (Kenny and Byron) care about each other? How can you tell? Do either of them treat Joetta differently than their brother?
- Kenny's dad tells them that because they are driving through the Deep South they can't just stop anywhere. Why is that?
- After Byron saves Kenny from the "Wool Pooh" he hugs him and cries. Were you surprised by that? What does it tell you about Byron?
- Kenny says a few times that he can't understand how people can hate so much. Toward the end of the book, Byron said he doesn't know but, "I think they just let hate eat them up and turn them into monsters." How do you think someone becomes so hate-filled? Do you think people are born that way? Do you think if a child grows up with hate-filled parents, they can avoid becoming hate-filled? How?

QUESTIONS FOR PONYO:

- At the beginning, Ponyo is caught up in a mass of ocean garbage. Ponyo's father says, "Humans are disgusting!" Do you think humans care enough about the Earth they live on? Do they take care of it well?

- Ponyo washes up where Sosuke is playing. Do you think he takes care of her well? In what way?
- Is Ponyo's father good or bad? Explain.
- Sosuke says to his father, "I'm taking care of everyone, Dad." What, exactly is he trying to communicate to his father?
- Sosuke's mother goes to help the elderly in the storm and leaves Sosuke and Ponyo to watch over the house. What would you do in this situation?
- When he sees she is dying, Sosuke releases Ponyo to the ocean. What does this prove?
- Ponyo's mother decides that Sosuke has passed the test. What was the test?

6
Education
(Reverse the Cycle)

"Education is the most powerful weapon which you can use to change the world."
– Nelson Mandela

As a classroom teacher, I spent most of my time in 3rd grade. This a transition year when the kids are expected to become more independent with more responsibilities in and out of the classroom. Here they begin traversing the valley where silly fun will eventually be left behind in favor of "cool" fun. Cool fun is overrated, because the "cool" refers to what your peers think is cool, or – more specifically – what you think your peers will find cool. Boys and girls are constantly glancing about to see what the other kids think and how they're reacting to whatever just happened. Meanwhile, I worked like crazy to get them to hold onto the silly fun as long as possible, because I knew what was coming (and because I had learned that being cool and following the crowd are mutually exclusive).

It's occurring to me as I write this that most, if not all, of my most meaningful connections I made with students were NOT during formal instruction time. In fact, they weren't part of any lesson. They were conversations or parts of conversations in the between times - transitions, lunch, snack, morning arrival, afternoon pack-up,...etc. These meaningful connections would allow me to reach my students on a level independent of tests or grades or any kind of evaluation. It was a way to reach from trusted adult to open-minded child, and there's no better environment for modeling and teaching, compassion, equality and how to connect with others.

Ricardo Gonzalez stresses the impact of a positive student-teacher relationship:
"The student/teacher relationship is a cornerstone in a student's social maturation process. Cultivating a positive rapport with a non-parental authority figure allows students to define themselves, adapt to their environment and grow their emotional and social intelligence."

I developed the habit of chatting with second graders at lunch in the cafeteria, knowing they'd be my students the following year. Establishing a strong student/teacher connection was best done, I found, when the students were relaxed and more likely to have their guard down, which meant not during regular class time. It was these times, when more casual interactions allowed them to be more open and honest - more authentic. It was during these times when they would be more likely to speak from the heart, and I needed only to listen.

Education should focus on students as human beings and individuals, rather than as participants in a contest. Many principals and parents alike are more commonly focused on increasing individual grades and school scores, rather than on growing minds and self-expression. I recall only *one* principal I worked under who truly reflected this in his priorities and how he ran the school.

In today's generic, standards-based school climate, this non-soul-crushing model of education is rare. To their credit, there are many teachers who practice educating their students in a way that welcomes multiple perspectives and plenty of self-expression. Book club talks can go a long way towards supplementing the healthy discussion the kids are missing out on in other classrooms.

In the absence of a school or at least one teacher's classroom, where the students can regularly and authentically express themselves without fear of imperfect grades or straying from the norm, it's up to parents to find a way to provide the genuine brand of life-education that a quality book club can offer.

The boy-girl gap clearly widens during the third grade year, and I find it to be for the worse. Boys are becoming more "concerned" with sports and prowess, as well as more vocal about their identities and successes. My input as the teacher carried very little weight. I was uncool by definition, so I could only – artificially – force issues such as gender stereotypes into the light. But I still tried like hell to make my students think seriously about that sort of thing. It was always apparent to them that I didn't follow professional football (or any sports besides the Olympic Games), and that I liked all kinds of music and theatre and the color pink and whatever else that was even vaguely attributed to the female gender.

School is such a significant part of childhood and developing perspective, that even the slightest dismissal – by us as parents – of what goes on there (inside the classrooms and out) is an opportunity for stereotyping and group mentality to creep in. Or maybe I should say, takeover.

I cringe whenever I hear a teacher separating boys and girls for any reason. It's bad enough when they do it for some sort of academic (or athletic) competition, but how about when they do it for "learning" purposes? There's no significant long-term concrete evidence that points to an advantage in grouping boys and girls separately. It is evident, on the other hand, that separating boys and girls -at the very least – keeps them from learning to communicate effectively.

At the worst it feeds the misconception of some fundamental difference which doesn't even exist. The misconception is continuously fed with adult sanctioned behavior.

"Boys spend their time with other boys, sealing the boys-will-be-boys prophecy; girls hang out with other girls, honing one another's chatty, cautious and decidedly pink preference in clothes and accessories. Researchers call it gender intensification..." - Lise Eliot

Boys and girls share all the skills required to succeed in school, regardless of slightly varying developmental tendencies. Diversity in everything from reading partners to research teams is bound to raise the level of learning. This goes for all grades. Children are keen (mentally fit and flexible) to take on new information. We must not force them to stereotype simply because it's what we are accustomed to.

"In 2005, researchers found that mathematically inclined girls whose fathers believed females aren't "wired" for the subject were less interested in pursuing it."
- Peggy Orenstein

Highly effective adult problem-solving teams almost always consist of both men and women. Why not give them consistent opportunities to work and play together as children? This way they can learn to value one another's strengths, rather than feeding the misconception that they are too different to cooperate successfully.

TEACHERS, the next time you're about to separate your students into groups of boys and girls, please consider the following from *Pink Brain, Blue Brain*, by Lise Eliot Ph.D.:

"The more similar boys' and girls' activities are, the more similar their brains will be."

*"Nearly all of the evidence for sex differences in the brain comes from studies of **adult** men and women."*

Also Teachers, please accept and teach Science, because – whether male or female:

"[S]tudents' ignorance about evolution will seriously undermine their understanding of the world and the natural laws governing it, and their introduction to other explanations described as 'scientific' will give them false ideas about scientific methods and criteria."
— Central Conference of American Rabbis

I'm choosing not to write a whole section on school shootings, not because I'm naive enough to to think that ignoring them will make them stop happening – there's just nothing to be said other than that they must stop. Our children require – at the very least – to attend school without danger or fear of getting hurt, let alone murdered. Let us follow the lead of the Parkland students– and all students– to let *people* talk and instigate REAL CHANGE, and **not** let money talk.

Childhood is the time to strike a chord within our children for equality and the inherent cooperation and positive behavior that will ensue. We, as dads, need to step up our input, since schools are populated with more female adult role models (especially in the more crucial early years). I have taught in many schools where the male role models were so limited... the principal, and/or the PE teacher, and/or one or 2 token classroom teachers. The rest were all women. Even if they're top notch teachers, it's an erroneous message for the male students that says "This isn't really where you belong." -or- "Your time here is merely a formality." When you don't see yourself represented in your school, you get the message that teaching or taking care of young children is not something that men can do.

THE BECHDEL TEST

Anytime you watch a movie or TV show (or read a book!), see if it passes The Bechdel Test.

Alison Bechdel's comic strip *Dykes To Watch Out For* first mentioned the three criteria, which is now referred to as The Bechdel Test.

To pass The Bechdel Test, the piece must meet these three criteria:
1. The movie has to have at least two women in it,
2. who talk to each other,
3. about something besides a man.

To go further, some have said the characters must be named and the conversation must last at least 60 seconds.

Go! Test your entertainment.

BOOK RECOMMENDATIONS
on the topic of Education

3rd graders	~**In the Footsteps of Crazy Horse** by Joseph Marshall III ~Harry Potter and the Sorcerer's Stone by J.K. Rowling ~Series of Unfortunate Events: The Bad Beginning by Lemony Snicket
6th graders	~**The Best Man** by Richard Peck ~Hatchet by Gary Paulsen

Movies/ TV	• **Harry Potter and the Sorcerer's Stone (2001)** • Series of Unfortunate Events (Netflix series, 2017-) • The Karate Kid (1984) • School Ties (1992)

REMINDER:
Pre-read or skim the books to decide which ones will work best for your particular group and the current ages of the boys. While some of the books on the list for older kids might be okay for your group, some of the lower level books may also work well for an issue that an older group is grappling with. These

suggestions are flexible - a jumping off point to get the dialogue started. I included issues that I strongly feel we must address, but the topics all overlap from one chapter to the next, since they share the same underlying themes.

QUESTIONS FOR IN THE FOOTSTEPS OF CRAZY HORSE:

- After reading this book, we learn that a lot of what is written in history is written by the "winners" and there may be another side of the story. What could this mean about textbooks?
- Why is it important to know our ancestors' history? Do you want your great-great-grandchildren to know your story?
- Grandpa says, "Animals and people don't understand each other anymore... people began to think they were better than anything." What did he mean?
- Grandpa says, "There were a lot of good and brave warriors... But not all of them were really good men." What made Crazy Horse a good man? What made him a good leader?
- Grandpa says war is sad no matter what side you are on. Do you think war can be good? Why or why not?
- What do you think has changed for Jimmy at the end of the book that makes his bullies walk away?

- How much does each one of Archer's teachers impact his experience at school? How much can one teacher change your entire school experience?
- The book begins by saying "boys aren't too interested in weddings". Is that a stereotype?
- When Archer ripped his pants open, the adults at the wedding laughed and took pictures. What do you think of that response?
- Why do you think Archer feels that, "In grade school, your best friend better never be a girl unless you *are* a girl"?
- What do you think of all the bullying that happens in the boys' bathroom in Archer's elementary school? What would you do in those situations?
- Archer says, "Kids know things before their grown-ups know they know." Is this is true?
- Have you ever had a lockdown in your school? Were you scared? What would have to happen so kids wouldn't have to do lockdowns anymore?
- It's interesting that so many parents started volunteering and sending brownies when Mr. McLeod came. Do you think the same would have happened if the student teacher was a woman?
- Did Mr. McLeod do a good job handling Russell's bullies? Do you think it was good that he came out to the students? Did he make an impact on anyone by his actions?
- Do you agree with Archer's dad that guys don't talk about their feelings? Archer says many times to different people in his life that he needs things spelled out for him. How could it

be more helpful if the grownups talked about their feelings?
- Hilary came to their school with a lot of confidence and self-worth, even in a wheelchair with a "girl's name"- What did that do for the school and for Archer?
- Do you think all of Archer's questions to Uncle Paul about love and Mr.McLeod are what helps them get together again? Why?

QUESTIONS FOR HARRY POTTER:

- How does Harry fit in to the Dursley family? How do the Dursleys justify Harry's role?
- Why does Harry say "We'll take the lot!" when the lady on the Hogwarts Express asks if they want anything off the trolley?
- What does Draco mean when he tells Harry that he can help him determine who is the right sort of wizard?
- How does Ron respond to Hermione the first several times they interact, before they become friends? How is it different from how Harry responds to her?
- What class/classes would you most want to take if you went to Hogwarts?
- How does Harry's home with the Dursley's compare with his sense of belonging at Hogwarts?
- What might it be like to have teachers who are responsible for you outside the classroom?

7
Consent
(Listen with Ears and Eyes)

"...More than half of all rape victims are assaulted by the age of eighteen..."
-Jackson Katz

I had a colleague who regularly greeted 8-year-olds as they walked into the classroom with "Where's my hug?" This is a dreadful question for a kid who doesn't want to hug his teacher, and also doesn't want to disappoint her. Children aren't stuffed animals, but some grown-ups are so taken with them, they forget about personal space.

My son had a classmate who hugged him everyday at preschool, just because she liked him. He would stand with his arms at his side and wait for it to be over. Meanwhile some other parents would say how cute it was and even chuckle at his obvious discomfort. After all, it was so cute and the little girl was only expressing harmless affection. No physical contact that is not one hundred percent accepted by both people is harmless. And I hate it for all the times my little boy had to stand there and not complain – just because the big people gave him no option to act on his feelings, even though they allowed the little girl to act on hers. What might this have taught him about what's okay to do to other people's bodies?

Consent is an issue for both genders. It needs to be okay for boys to say "no" as well. My son has a friend at school with whom he's very close, and they love to hug each other. But, this doesn't automatically extend to everyone else at school. This is the one person at school he is comfortable with anything more than a handshake or high five. This was established by both boys' mothers talking to them about what made them comfortable.

We should encourage our kids to be kind and compassionate in an equitable way. But that doesn't mean forcing them to hug or kiss anyone (including relatives) out of politeness. Consent should not be a luxury, and children deserve to choose for themselves if and when they offer theirs.

Other than a handshake, a high-five, or perhaps a pat on the back – we all require some kind of undeniable consent before touching someone else's body. Silence is not consent. If the consent isn't crystal clear, there's no consent. If someone consents, then changes her or his mind, there's no consent. You may roll your eyes, or think, "It's just a hug!", but, as Tracee Ellis Ross explained,

"...Some of you are wondering what the connection is between the innocuous and the horrific. Two things that seem to be on opposite ends of the spectrum. Well, the common thread IS the spectrum. The innocuous makes space for the horrific."

How well we listen often dictates the success of our relationships. It's never too early to develop this ability, yet boys are commonly behind in this area. The importance of creating a culture of listening can't be overstated. Our own ability to read those around us is key to communication. Good listening skills are more than half of good communication. Getting our boys listening to girls while they're still young will go a long way toward helping them become allies as adults. True allies support, regardless of peer pressure or outside expectation. True allies are nurturers.

Says Nora Samaran, *"The opposite of masculine rape culture is masculine nurturance culture: men increasing their capacity to nurture, and becoming whole... when you google 'man comforting a woman' many of the top hits are about women comforting men ...'how to comfort a guy, how to comfort a man when he's stressed, how to comfort a guy when he's upset.' Apparently lots and lots of people on planet earth are googling how to comfort men... and fewer are googling how to comfort women... Could it be that a lot of men have no models for how to nurture, comfort, soothe, and thus strengthen people they care about? "*

Programmed to have their own needs satisfied, children face an uphill battle when it comes to interpreting the needs of others. They see adults interacting, and take their cues from them. Listening is a skill of stamina, developed over years. Ideally, we should listen at least as much as we talk (this is rare, even among adults). Listening is observing with our eyes, too. When we pay attention, we can read someone's facial expression or body language and interpret that as valid, fully addmisable communication. But we have to be looking at someone in order to see their sad eyes when they say they're "happy", and know which to believe. Even grown-ups (more likely men than women) can be notoriously bad at this.

It's human nature to please other people. People prefer to avoid saying "no". People also prefer to avoid situations where they may have to say "no." We are therefore likely to refrain from putting others on the spot. So, silence is often the first message. Silence - in this case - means "no".

When 1 in 6 women is raped or sexually assaulted, someone is doing that raping. We must own the reality that rape is a men's issue.

On RAINN's website, they explain, *"...consent is about communication. And it should happen every time. Giving consent for one activity, one time, does not mean giving consent for increased or recurring sexual contact. For example, agreeing to kiss someone doesn't give that person permission to remove your clothes. Having sex with someone in the past doesn't give that person permission to have sex with you again in the future."*

An extremely disturbing aspect of rape is that most men who commit sexual assault do not truly process that they have done it. In the 2017 *New York Times* Article, "What Experts Know About Men Who Rape", Heather Murphy reports:

"Men who rape tend to start young, in high school or the first couple years of college, likely crossing the line with someone they know."

Men who score high in empathy are less likely and men who score high in narcissism are more likely to commit sexual assault.

"Most subjects in these studies freely acknowledge non-consensual sex- but that does not mean they consider it real rape."

Asked "if they had penetrated against their consent," said Dr. Koss, the subject will say yes. Asked if he did "something like rape," the answer is almost always no.

IT'S NOT JUST THE JOCKS

There's no single, specific group of boys that needs to be targeted for consent training. Frankly, all boys are potential rapists. I realize how bad that sounds, but we are here because this is serious. There are groups out there right now actively working against equality. "Men's Rights" groups, Incels, The Manosphere (I'll touch on this in Chapter 9)- are all working to divide the sexes. We need to understand that our focus for connecting and empowering our collective youth extends to every type and personality of boy. Consider the following account from a self-proclaimed nerd:

In his piece, "Your Princess is in Another Castle: Misogyny, Entitlement, and Nerds", Arthur Chu says,

"We (male) nerds grow up force-fed this script. Lusting after women "out of our league" was what we did... This is, to put it mildly, a problematic attitude to grow up with. Fixating on a woman from afar and then refusing to give up when she acts like she's not interested is, generally, something that ends badly for everyone involved. But it's a narrative that nerds and nerd media kept repeating... But the overall problem is one of a culture where instead of seeing women as, you know, people, protagonists of

their own stories just like we are of ours, men are taught that women are things to "earn," to "win." That if we try hard enough and persist long enough, we'll get the girl in the end. Like life is a video game and women, like money and status, are just part of the reward we get for doing well. So what happens to nerdy guys who keep finding out that the princess they were promised is always in another castle? When they "do everything right," they get good grades, they get a decent job, and that wife they were promised in the package deal doesn't arrive? When the persistent passive-aggressive Nice Guy act fails, do they step it up to elaborate Steve-Urkel-esque stalking and stunts? Do they try elaborate Revenge of the Nerds-style ruses? Do they tap into their inner John Galt and try blatant, violent rape?"

A WORD ON PORNOGRAPHY

Did you know the average age for a boy to first see pornography is 11 years old? How about the fact that 1 in 10 children have accidentally seen porn? This is undoubtedly a super-unhealthy way to learn about relationships and sex. Yet many of our boys are learning about relationships from pornography.

"New research from the security technology company Bitdefender, has reported children under the age of 10 now account for 22% of online porn consumption under 18 -years old. Particularly alarming is that the sites most visited by children under 10 include porn mega sites like Pornhub. The under 10 age group is now accounting for one in 10 visitors to porn video sites, per Bitdefender."

-Kristin MacLaughlin, NetNanny

Constant viewing of graphic sexual acts can desensitize boys (or anyone) to the intimate, private, human nature of physical relationships. At some point, the partner is perceived more as a means to an end. Having their young brains register women as objects is dangerous. Seeing unhealthy, unrealistic models of what sex should look like leaves boys poorly prepared for contact, let alone relationships with real partners.

"10% of children in the 7th grade have stated that they are watching enough porn to be concerned that they may have an addiction issue and not be able to stop. Many experts believe this is due to two primary issues: mobile accessibility and desensitization at an earlier age. "Young people are turning to the internet to learn about sex and relationships. We know they are frequently stumbling across porn, often unintentionally, and they are telling us very clearly that this is having a damaging and upsetting effect on them."
- Dame Esther Rantzen, founder of ChildLine

Joseph Gordon Levitt made a smart film (Don Jon, 2013) about pornography and how it keeps men from having true intimacy in real-life relationships. This could be a good film to talk about in book club in the late high school years. Levitt has been very candid on his experience and thoughts, *"We have a tendency in our culture to take people and treat them like things."*

Physical intimacy requires constant checking in with one's partner. If you're unsure whether your partner is okay with the level of contact, you must ask. Never assume that the other person consents. If – after inquiring – you're still unsure, assume the answer is "No".

BOOK RECOMMENDATIONS
on the topic of Consent

3rd graders	~**Let's Talk About Body Boundaries, Consent & Respect** by Jayneen Sanders
6th graders	~**What Does Consent Really Mean?** (graphic novel) by Pete Wallis & Thalia Wallis

Movies/ TV	• **YouTube Video:** **"Consent: It's Simple as Tea"** (Clean version, 2015) • The Princess Bride (1987)

REMINDER:
Pre-read or skim the books to decide which ones will work best for your particular group and the current

ages of the boys. While some of the books on the list for older kids might be okay for your group, some of the lower level books may also work well for an issue that an older group is grappling with. These suggestions are flexible - a jumping off point to get the dialogue started. I included issues that I strongly feel we must address, but the topics all overlap from one chapter to the next, since they share the same underlying themes.

QUESTIONS FOR LET'S TALK ABOUT BODY BOUNDARIES, CONSENT & RESPECT:

***This book has an amazing two-page guide in the back with really thoughtful and helpful questions-- I recommend you use that guide.

Make sure you ask:

- What does it mean that your body belongs to you?
- Are you allowed to say "no" to a hug?
- What have you learned from this book?

QUESTIONS FOR WHAT DOES CONSENT REALLY MEAN?:

***This book also has a terrific and comprehensive six-page Discussion Guide at the back of the book. Definitely make sure to ask:

- How would you describe consent and why is it important?

- Is porn a good way to learn about relationships?
- What did you learn about consent from this book?

QUESTIONS FOR CONSENT: IT'S SIMPLE AS TEA:

- Does the importance of consent make more sense after seeing the tea metaphor animated?
- Do you have any questions about consent?

8
LGBTQ

"We have to be able to talk about sexuality and identity in a nonhysterical way."
-Juno Dawson

After winning a bronze medal in Figure Skating at the 2018 Winter Olympic Games in PyeongChang, South Korea, Adam Rippon became the first openly gay athlete from the USA to win a medal at the Winter Olympics. In an interview with Ellen DeGeneres, he said that "1 in 5 kids today identifies with some sort of LGBTQ (IAGNC) identity." **1 in 5... which means the likelihood that either your son or one of his friends will identify as LGBTQ is pretty high.** Adam currently works with GLAAD to help "advance equality and accelerate acceptance for LGBTQ youth."

Let's face it, people have strong, often loud opinions about this topic, so it's tempting to put the discussion aside. But being uncomfortable is part of having tough conversations. If this is a tough conversation for you, good for you for tackling it on behalf of the young boys you're reaching out to. We also need to teach them that it's really important to bring things up that are important to them, even if they may be upsetting to others.

First, let's refresh ourselves on what the acronym stands for: Lesbian, gay, bisexual, transgender, queer/questioning (one longer version is: LGBTQIAGNC: Lesbian, gay, bisexual, transgender, queer, intersex, asexual, and gender-non-conforming).

It's well known (at least it should be) that individuals who identify as LGBTQ (or somewhere within the longer acronym) have lived within communities, as part of human society since the earliest recorded or documented time. This is significant. This tells us that, regardless of differences between those who are LGBTQ and those who are not, neither group is mutually exclusive, nor subject to denial of their rights. We have coexisted as members of the same society, since the origins of humanity. We must stop ostracizing members of societies on the sole basis that they don't match our personal definitions of gender. Thank goodness we are different.

"Just because LGBTQ people are in the minority, it doesn't mean they are not normal" - Juno Dawson

Now let's get to the kids: The Human Rights Campaign (you may recognize them by the yellow "equal" sign within a blue background) completed a survey of over 10,000 LGBTQ youth (13 - 17 year olds), as part of their report - Growing Up LGBTQ in America. Their findings are "a call to action for all adults who want to ensure that young people can thrive." That call is meant for us - and it is one of the precise reasons we NEED to talk to our sons.

Jack Drescher, MD, Distinguished Fellow, American Psychiatric Association, Clinical Associate Professor of Psychiatry, New York Medical College - said the following about the survey:

"HRC's groundbreaking survey...exposes a sad state of affairs...today's LGBTQ youth are still members of the only minority group "born into an enemy camp," subject to family and community disapproval and animus (hostility) rather than loving support...significant numbers of LGBTQ youth feel unwelcome it their own communities, ...many of them believe that the only way to ever find acceptance is by escaping from the places where they grew up and to leave friends and family behind."

As a parent, this is truly heartbreaking. There's no way this is getting swept under the rug. We owe it to our sons to ask them their perspective on this and discuss steps we will take to turn this tragic reality (especially considering how far we've supposedly come since the civil rights movement) around in our own circles.

How can we address this on a daily basis? Let's start with how we talk about them. Consistently referring to the LGBTQ community as a completely disassociated and disparate group is a way of marginalizing everyone who identifies as LGBTQ. It implies that they are utterly separate from "non-LGBTQ" folk, or – ...the "rest" of us. This is obviously not the case. We would do well to back-up and recognize that most communities overlap and connect in ways that are inextricable from one another. It would be beneficial, for example, if we would seek out more first person accounts of news and information from within their community. We could then establish a more "us" or "we" focused perspective. This attitude could empower those within and without the community.

Simply put, individuals who identify as LGBTQ deserve to be fully accepted and respected, as do individuals in all communities according to the last line of the Pledge of Allegiance ("with Liberty and Justice for all"). At some point we must embrace the fact that we are ultimately all one community.

Wade Davis II, the former NFL player who came out in 2016 said to the Billings Gazette: *"What I think that's about* (a Billings City Council vote against an anti-discrimination law), *honestly, it's fear-based...I really think that, if you look at our history, whenever there has been a shift in progress around any type of social issue, there's always a pushback, because I think we're resistant as mankind to change."*

And in his 2016 Ted Talk "The Mask of Masculinity, Wade Davis also says, *"... the root of homophobia is really sexism. And ...until women are free, men can never be free. And then, we must do the work to start loving ourselves."*

Just to keep it real, here are some statistics about school-aged children from our country's National PTA website:

- In 2013, 74% of LGBT students were verbally harassed (called names or threatened) because of their sexual orientation, and 55% because of their gender expression

- 30% of LGBT students reported missing at least one entire day in the past month because they felt unsafe or uncomfortable at school, and 10.6% missed four days or more

We know this is happening all around us. We can't expect our own children to pass ignorantly by, while this is happening around them - OR - to them or their friends.

Clearly, we - as adults, caregivers, caretakers, and role models - need to pick up the torch of understanding and acceptance, the torch of humanity.

As a European-American (a term I never use), I hold strong beliefs about my citizenship, as well as pride in my ancestors (mainly for surviving). But it doesn't hurt or offend me if someone of alternate ancestry holds differing beliefs. Coexisting with people whose skin doesn't exactly match mine is not demeaning, insulting or blasphemous. I don't need to focus on our differences in order to accept them. I celebrate and embrace our shared humanity. We've learned, after all, that diversity within any group broadens perspective and increases the potential for success. Just as there is strength in diversity, there is danger in homogeneity.

> "If we teach the habit of
> first acknowledging
> our similarities
> with others,
> the labels that have kept
> them and us separate
> will take on
> less and less
> significance."

So, the first label we apply should be that of human/brother/sister – or whatever term conveys the commonality we share with all humans who inhabit our planet. If we teach the habit of first acknowledging our similarities, the labels that have kept us separate will take on less and less significance. As that happens, negative labels used to alienate communities, such as LGBTQ and others will cease to impact our viewing of them as "them" instead of us. Because, ultimately, they are us.

As role models, we must constantly be working to ensure that our young ones feel loveable, exactly the way they are. Just imagine Mr. Rogers talking to them. You know he's right.

It should be noted that children as young as 3 years old have shown awareness that their mind gender doesn't match their body gender. Imagine how many children spend years with no one to open up to or relate to and no example to follow that says "YOU DON'T HAVE TO CHANGE TO BE ACCEPTED. THE ONLY RIGHT WAY TO BE YOURSELF IS TO BE WHO YOU TRULY FEEL YOU ARE, ON THE INSIDE." It's essential to let our boys know it's okay to be who they are, so they can internalize it, and communicate that to their friends.

TEACHING OUR SONS TO BE ALLIES

No time is "too early" to talk about these things. The mistake would be in waiting. Imagine your son knowing he's "different" from an early age and keeping it hidden, whether from shame, fear or confusion. Let your son know that you would accept him if he is LGBTQ. Just as importantly, if he is not- teach him what it means to be an LGBTQ ally. **This is the mission of this chapter.**

How do we answer their questions exactly? Perhaps you aren't 100% certain how you feel, or maybe your own parents had homophobic views. This is why having book club can be such a gift. If necessary, let another dad you trust take the reins- while you're still in the room, part of it. Or explain, as Lin-Manuel Miranda said so simply, "Love is love is love is love is love is love is love." Sometimes boys love boys. Sometimes girls love girls. The important thing is to choose someone who cares about you and respects you.

I cringe when I see parents calling a boy and girl toddler "boyfriend and girlfriend"... First of all, it sends a subtle message that this is the default relationship of male and female- rather than simple friendship. Since we know (from Chapter 2 & 7) that fostering friendships between boys and girls helps battle rape culture, these comments aren't as cute as they seem on the surface. But, I also cringe because they've labeled their child's sexuality by default.

I've heard my wife ask my 5-year-old son, "Do you think you'll marry a girl, or a boy, or no one?" Why not let them know all the possibilities are open? In this way, they know our expectations of them are simply for them to be thoughtful about their choices. In asking broad questions, they will hear our acceptance of them no matter who they turn out to be.

As for teaching your kids to be LGBTQ allies, this book club is a great start. In her article, "7 Ways To Teach Your Kids To Be LGBT Allies", Angela Johnson lists: *"Step 1 - Turn To A Book, and Step 2 - Talk about it."*

Reading books with LGBTQ characters is a great way to start the discussion. (When you begin introducing female protagonists into the mix, make sure to read *My Mixed Up Berry Blue Summer*, by Jennifer Gennari.) Ask them what they would do in the character's position, etc. What would they do if a kid is bullied at school? Do you have stories from your youth you can share about how LGBTQ students were treated? Was it more of a secret? Share your stories as well as what you wish you'd have done differently, or what actions you were proud to have taken.

BOOK RECOMMENDATIONS
on the topic of LGBTQ

3rd graders	~**The Story of Red** by Michael Hall ~I Am Jazz by Jessica Herthel & Jazz Jennings
6th graders	~**Gracefully Grayson** by Ami Polonsky ~Marco Impossible by Hannah Moskowitz ~George by Alex Gino

Movies/ TV	• **A Big LGBT Thank You to President Obama, The Ellen Show (2017)** • Freak Show (2018) • Shrek: The Musical (2008) • Queer Eye (Netflix, 2018–)

REMINDER:

Pre-read or skim the books to decide which ones will work best for your particular group and the current ages of the boys. While some of the books on the list for older kids might be okay for your group, some of the lower level books may also work well for an issue that an older group is grappling with. These suggestions are flexible - a jumping off point to get the dialogue started. I included issues that I strongly feel we must address, but the topics all overlap from one chapter to the next, since they share the same underlying themes.

QUESTIONS FOR THE STORY OF RED:

- All of the crayons have labels. Why? Should people have labels? Why or why not?
- Why didn't Red notice that he wasn't red? Why didn't the other crayons notice that he wasn't red?
- Who should decide what to write on a label? Should they be able to change it, once it's been written?
- Why couldn't Red change his color? What can we change about ourselves? What can we not change?
- What would you write on your own label?

QUESTIONS FOR GRACEFULLY GRAYSON:
*Because Grayson doesn't ever use self-identifying

pronouns in the book, I will respectfully use the "they" pronoun here.

- Why do you think Grayson eats in the library?
- What changes for Grayson when they become friends with Amelia?
- What qualities make Mr. Finn "one of the best teachers" at the school? Why do you think the students love him so much?
- Why do you think Grayson signs up to audition for the play?
- Once Grayson gets the part of Persephone, some kids aren't supportive-- but the other kids in their cast are supportive. Why do you think that is?
- Do you think Mr. Finn is treated fairly? Why or why not?
- What was your reaction to Grayson's mom's letters?
- Grayson's aunt and uncle reacted very differently to the letters. How did their reactions make Grayson feel?
- Paige's mom (Marla) tells Grayson, "...we want you to know that you are welcome at our house anytime you need anything." Is that important for Grayson to hear?
- What if Grayson had never auditioned for the play?

QUESTIONS FOR A BIG LGBT THANK YOU TO PRESIDENT OBAMA:

- Do you know anyone who is LGBTQ?
- Have you ever doubted yourself?

- If a friend told you they were LGBTQ, how could you support them?
- Do you have at least one adult and one friend you could share your feelings with if you were struggling with something big like identity?
- Do you think things can get better when you are older? Why?

9
Social Media & Technology

*"Like trying to make clothes fit that are way too big,
children will use social media inappropriately until they
are older and it fits them better."*
-Adrian H. Wood, Ph.D.

As a kid in the 70's, I would go out the front door (or the back door) and be free of the boring confines of "nothing to do" in moments. I could walk to the train tracks, the pond, the school playground, Baskin & Robbins Ice Cream, or I could turn on Rocatan, the closest dead-end street where kids would play in the middle of the road since cars never drove too fast. I brought nothing with me. No phone, no headphones, no watch - zero. I usually found something fun to do. Plus, although I never thought about it this way as a child, I spent time connecting with the living world around me.

Zip forward a mere 40 years and...

> *"Children aged five to 16 spend an*
> *average of six and a half hours a day in front of a*
> *screen...according to market research firm Childwise.*
> *Teen-aged boys spend the longest, with an average of*
> *eight hours."*
> -Jane Wakefield, BBC News

...And that was three years ago! This is just crazy to me. But we can't go backwards. Children can't recall a time when there was no internet.   We need to accept that the internet and online access has changed the way that kids interact with the world around them – including their families.

As I write this in 2018, the average age for a child to receive their first smartphone is ten. No test or online education is required of a child before they are handed an adult-ready computer that can access all kinds of information and potentially endanger or harm them. Some parents assume user controls and blocks make it safe enough for their child to go unmonitored. Some trust their child's judgement, so they don't even bother setting limits. I strongly advocate against this. As in many situations, it's our job as parents to find out as much as we can about possible dangers (especially when something's relatively new-- We are the first generation of parents truly dealing with technology on this level) and then make an informed decision (and then change our minds if necessary, upon receipt of new information).

There are some books that really drive home the idea of social media gone terribly wrong for teens, but they are for more of a high school audience. If you are at that age, look up *The Future of Us* by Jay Asher and Carolyn Mackler and *Need* by Joelle Charbonneau.

Let's acknowledge the vacuum factor. The way social media can suck your mind away from the here and now, then inundate you with words and images while you sit passively mezmorized...

This cannot be overstated: Limit screen time.

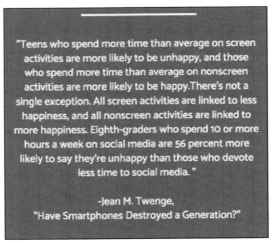

"Teens who spend more time than average on screen activities are more likely to be unhappy, and those who spend more time than average on nonscreen activities are more likely to be happy. There's not a single exception. All screen activities are linked to less happiness, and all nonscreen activities are linked to more happiness. Eighth-graders who spend 10 or more hours a week on social media are 56 percent more likely to say they're unhappy than those who devote less time to social media."

-Jean M. Twenge,
"Have Smartphones Destroyed a Generation?"

Our kids don't have the luxury - as many of us did - of some or all of their childhood being social media free. A big part of Media Literacy Education (a necessary requirement for kids and adults) is learning how not to drown in the onslaught of images and words that are constantly paraded before us on a multitude of ever-present screens.

We have no choice but to somehow tackle this media jungle because as parents of young children we can't just ignore it.

Why can't we ignore it? Sex and violence, for starters.

No, I don't think video games or the internet directly cause violence. But many men on these screens are represented as perpetrators of violence. Or, as Jackson Katz puts it...

"Violent masculinity is a cultural norm."

Our sons can be subjected to images and videos where men are behaving violently, often towards women. I'm sure you're aware -on some level - of the possible scenarios in Grand Theft Auto (just to name a single example- in this game most of the women are strippers or prostitutes and in some cases you can get a reward for killing them).

"They found that boys who played the games containing sexism and violence were more likely to identify with the character they were playing. They also reported less empathy toward the images of female victims."
-Alexandra Sifferlin, "Here's What Sexist Video Games Do to Boys' Brains"

We have to talk about this violent imagery with our children and establish it as unrealistic and wrong. We must reinforce the fact that online material, and subject matter in many video games is often populated with unacceptable role models.

Sex, more specifically, pornography is highly accessible online and has been for years.

"What is new is the degree to which children's sexualized bodies are on display in the media"
– Jackson Katz

Parents and teachers alike need to pick up the torch and light the way for children as they attempt to navigate the unavoidable digital realm...

"In order to help people analyze or deconstruct media messages, educators need to bring the images... into the classroom." – Jackson Katz

DIGITAL CITIZENSHIP

"Just as students have to learn how to be good citizens within their community, they need to know how to behave and be a positive part of the digital community. Digital citizenship is an important responsibility that everyone needs to understand as it encapsulates as many aspects of behavior and actions as physical interaction does. Depending on the age of the student, there are different areas that you can focus on... Starting with

stranger danger and cyberbullying, your students will need to continue to learn about this aspect of technology throughout their educational career."
-Matthew Lynch

I worked in a school that incorporated a Digital Citizenship program into the curriculum, beginning in Kindergarten. It was good for initially creating an awareness, even in the early grades (K-2) that we have to "behave" online. Then it was good for establishing a norm of double checking everything internet/social media related, as students gained more and more independence with their school work. Ultimately it helped students find a balance between all those multiple screens and good old fashioned paper and pencil work. Keep in mind, digital citizenship programs and requirements must be constantly updated and readdressed, since social media is being constantly updated and re-invented – more with marketing in mind and less with concern for student needs (or, for that matter, needs of any consumer of social media).

In addition, we can't expect children to decipher the misrepresentations of male versus female roles in society as they are often seen online.

"A crucial [part] of the patriarchal system is the gender ideology that is transmitted to young people through media." -Jackson Katz

I'm constantly struck by the common knowledge of useless crap that exists solely because of Facebook (Instagram, Twitter,... insert whatever platform that comes to mind here). Wasting our time on this stuff is disturbing because meanwhile we are missing many of the meaningful messages in the material we're scrolling through.

Another aspect of this scrolling is The Comparison Game-- on social media not only are you scrolling and comparing your life to everyone else's-- you are comparing it to the most perfect parts of their lives they are sharing. People get stuck comparing their worst moments to other people's best moments. If most adults can't reconcile this inconsistency, we certainly cannot expect kids to interpret it in a healthy way... yet another reason kids don't need social media.

Dax Shepard interviewed his wife Kristen Bell on his podcast, *Armchair Expert*, and a portion of their conversation where they talked about social media sums it up:

Dax: That's something that you and I talk about a ton which is comparing yourself to people.

Kristen: Right, I don't want a comparison hangover, you get comparison hangovers... It's useless and it's a waste of fucking time.

Dax: It doesn't really matter what you've done or accomplished in your life, you will definitely be able to find someone who's much better at whatever thing...

Kristen: ...and now we live in the age of social media where you truly see the best of the best and everyone feels less than.

THE MANOSPHERE

I hadn't even heard of The Manosphere before researching for this book. It's equally absurd and horrifying. It's important to bring this up with our sons, even at an early age. If we warn them that this is out there and why it is dangerous, when they come upon it they will be less likely to be drawn in by a friend who just claims it's "funny" or "entertaining".

The manosphere is *"the amorphous, fractious constellation of online men's groups united in their belief that feminism is ruining the world"* - Peter Baker

Some of the most recent domestic terrorist attacks have been committed by men who call themselves "incels", involuntary celibates who feel sex is owed to them. Their hatred for women is cited in their attacks.

This online rabbit hole is something we need our sons to be aware of and learn to work against. Young men are drawn in with overtures of shared disappointment and commiseration, and offers of the path to "getting what is owed to them".
Awareness is key. We must be constantly aware ourselves and teach our sons to be wary of the many online underground groups who rely on boys having no one to talk to (this is EXACTLY where father-son book clubs come in).

DO IT FOR YOUR HEALTH AND THEIR HEALTH

"Social media can cause teens to lose connection with family and instead view "friends" as their foundation. Since the cognitive brain is still being formed, the need for your teen to be attached to your family is just as important now as when they were younger... While they need attachments to their friends, they need healthy family attachment more." - Victoria L. Dunckley M.D.

Consider your proximity to your devices. Are they always on you or beside you? In our home, we set up a charging station for all devices (phones, iPads, mp3 players, laptops, etc). It's in the dining room, which happens to be the room of the house we go in LEAST and it's also the farthest from the bedrooms. We do our best to leave them all there unless we need them for something specific. Have a meeting and make a plan that works for your family- decide what your "screen goals" are and make a plan to get closer to those goals.

Meanwhile, we should ALL spend time getting lost in our "non-screen" hobbies. These activities often lead us to what we are good at and what we love. Rather than scrolling through screens, lose yourself in more tangible hobbies - reading, drawing, building, creating, playing an instrument,...etc. There are many activities that can engage the mind and give you a healthy sense of losing yourself in the moment (while actually growing your potential) with no electronics around.

A while back, this heartfelt piece went viral. It hits the nail on the head.   In Rachel Macy Stafford's piece, "Tether Yourself", she says to her daughter;

"But here's how you take back control: Awareness ... you see, awareness changes everything. Awareness is your weapon against the hidden influences and damaging behaviors. While you are online, your mind, your thoughts, your core values are drifting to wherever tech companies want you to go. The remedy is to limit the time you spend drifting in the online world and tether yourself to real life.

Tether yourself...To real people, real conversations, and real scenery. Tether yourself... To furry animals, interesting books, good music, the great outdoors. Tether yourself...To spatulas, hammers, cameras, paintbrushes, and yoga mats."

Experiment:
Weekly Screen Time Log

Are you spending more time on hobbies or screens?

Day	TV	Other screens (iPad, phones, computers)	Hobbies
Mon			
Tue			
Wed			
Thur			
Fri			
Sat			
Sun			
TOTAL=			

BOOK RECOMMENDATIONS
on the topic of Social Media & Technology

3rd graders	~**Blackout** by John Rocco
6th graders	~**You Go First** by Erin Entrada Kelly ~ #famous by Jilly Gagnon

| Movies/ TV | <ul><li>**How Social Media Makes Us Unsocial** (Allison Graham, Social Media Historian, Ted Talk) (2014)</li><li>Live My Digital for Students: Digital Footprint (YouTube) (2016)</li><li>Managing Your Online Reputation (Google for Education– YouTube) (2017)</li></ul> |

REMINDER:

Pre-read or skim the books to decide which ones will work best for your particular group and the current ages of the boys. While some of the books on the list for older kids might be okay for your group, some of the lower level books may also work well for an issue that an older group is grappling with. These suggestions are flexible – a jumping off point to get the dialogue started. I included issues that I strongly feel we must address, but the topics all overlap from one chapter to the next, since they share the same underlying themes.

- What does it mean to take something for granted? What do you take for granted?
- What brings the family together?
- What happens when they go outside?
- Is there a difference between talking to someone on the phone and talking to them in person? What's the difference?
- Why did the boy turn the lights back out at the end?

QUESTIONS FOR YOU GO FIRST:

- Ben says to Charlotte, "Do you think our generation relies too much on digital communication?" What do you think?
- Why do you think Ben and Lottie didn't share the truth with each other?
- Ben says, "Small talk is for small people." What do you think he means?
- Charlotte says she doesn't believe in changing things about yourself– you should be happy with who you are. Do you agree?
- Do you agree with Ben that "Adversity builds character"? Can you think you of a time when adversity in your own life made you stronger?
- When Charlotte goes into her backyard at midnight, she has her phone with her... do you think we should always have our phones nearby? Why or why not?
- Charlotte's mom was worried Ben was "a maniac from the internet". Can you

understand why she'd think that? Do you know any stories about people who pretended to be someone else online?

- The last chapter tells us that "researchers... found that having a healthy and reciprocal relationship with a friend can help alleviate emotional pain and improve physical health." What do you think having Wyatt and Magda as friends will do for Charlotte and Ben? Was it easier for them to be themselves with their in-person friend, or their online friend?

QUESTIONS FOR HOW SOCIAL MEDIA MAKES US UNHEALTHY:

- Are any of your family or friends addicted to their phone?
- Could you stay off screens for a whole day?
- Did you know texting while driving is the #1 cause of death for teens? Did that surprise you? How would you solve this problem?
- Would you consider making a plan with your family to be more mindful about screens (adults too!)?
- Has learning a bit about social media and screens changed your mind about how you want to use them? How?

10
Speaking Up & Speaking Out

*"...our need to belong can be the cause of our greatest
inhumanity... as it pushes us to say nothing when faced
with injustice, or to join in the abuse of people the group
has identified as different and therefore deserving of
unequal treatment."*
–Rosalind Wiseman

I went to school with Michael (I've changed his name),
who was often bullied. He was a little below average
size, and fairly quiet. For those reasons alone, he was
fair game to pick on. He was easy to ignore, push, cut
in front of and generally treat like an old,
uncherished, stuffed animal.

While I didn't actively participate in bullying Michael, I didn't speak up either. I don't recall ever interrupting when someone was being rude to him, or striking up a friendly conversation with him. My parents would have been appalled if I had ever bullied him, but they should have been equally appalled at how I stood by.

Of course, they didn't know about it. Things like that don't come up in conversations that are never had.

> "...It is more manly to take a stand for what is right than to blindly follow the majority..."
> -Jackson Katz

Not surprisingly, Michael became surly and cold, and he stayed that way through middle school and most of high school. It wasn't that he never smiled, but it certainly wasn't his default attitude.

This is one of the more tame cases. Sadly there are far worse tales to tell, if we bother to tell them. It's too late when they wind up on the news. There is no way to sugarcoat suicide or murder. Even before Columbine, there were sorrowful tales of the lives of boys with negligible opportunities for authentic self-expression coupled with access to weapons. We can do something about it. But it will take commitment.

"Reposition the bystander as... strong, courageous... not "uncool" or "narc"" - Jackson Katz

When our sons see us speaking out on behalf of others during book club, AND as part of our daily lives, they will then be prepared to do the same. For this to become the norm, we have to commit to building it. We can't just drop words on them and leave it at that. The ideas of brotherhood and manhood should be fueled with integrity and linked to humankind in general. We are not only teaching our sons to find positive ways to connect. We must also teach them to recognize the negative reasons people seek to unite, and work to eliminate them.

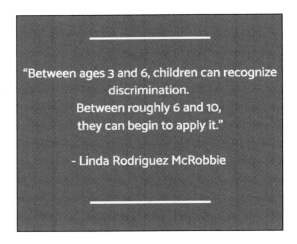

"Between ages 3 and 6, children can recognize discrimination.
Between roughly 6 and 10,
they can begin to apply it."

- Linda Rodriguez McRobbie

If this sounds like a lot, it is. But it starts with a conversation.

Teenage survivors of the Parkland massacre have boldly forced the conversation on our nation after being faced with the very worst of a boy. We need to hear them and reflect their urgency and value of humanity back towards our own children.

When 18-year-old David Hogg, one of the Parkland shooting survivors, began speaking up, he (along with other survivors) was faced with some horrible backlash (even death threats) from adults who refused to accept the horror and tragedy that David and his community had suffered. Rather than toning it down, or shutting up altogether (as some clearly preferred he would), he boldly used the attention to shine a light on minorities being affected by school gun violence who had previously been given no voice. When Hogg was asked about the media's biggest mistake in covering Stoneman Douglas, he responded, *"Not giving black students a voice. It's disgusting."*

At the very least, David Hogg, along with Emma Gonzalez and the other outspoken Parkland shooting survivors, are outstanding teenage role models for compassion and thoughtful action.

Between the time of the Columbine and Parkland shootings (19 years), there were many others (an estimated 200 school shootings in addition to numerous other shootings), but no real change. We mustn't allow silence to creep in again. Let's pull those teeth, if we must, and get people talking, beginning with our sons.

When they hear us yelling at a screen or radio about some news story, they should also see us calling, or emailing our representatives (it really doesn't take much time, and it's an outstanding way to show our kids we care). When we get some generic response about how the representative truly does "care", we can explain that each message of disappointment to an elected official is a reminder that "We are watching you!" ...the more they receive, the less they can go on ignoring us.

"Oftentimes kids are better at forcing change than adults. For many of us, as we age we grow more cautious, more measured; we feel like we have more to lose by speaking out. Kids, though, have an attuned sense of right and wrong and are just starting to form their world views."
–Kathleen Davis

In the past, people have been willing to let bad things happen to others because they didn't want to draw attention to themselves. Children are easily swayed to be silent. Even worse than peer pressure is "manhood" pressure, exerted even from afar whenever a man merely considers being compassionate.

Children can also be swayed to speak up more often in public, when it's the rule in their homes.

"When kids know their opinions count, they are more likely to talk out and feel comfortable speaking up for themselves. The best place for your child to learn to find his voice is in your home. Make sure that each of your kids has a chance to speak and be heard."
–Dr. Michele Borba

In case you were wondering, I have spotted "Michael", my childhood classmate, on Facebook. He's pictured in numerous locations with a family and a smile. He obviously has a strong heart. I have a feeling he's a loving dad.

BOOK RECOMMENDATIONS
on the topic of Speaking Up & Speaking Out

3rd graders	~**Hoot** by Carl Hiaasen
6th graders	~**The Epic Fail of Arturo Zamora** by Pablo Cartaya ~It's Your World by Chelsea Clinton

Movies/ TV	• **Selma (2014)** • The Odd Squad Movie (2016) • Spirited Away (2001) English version • Hoot (2006)

REMINDER:
Pre-read or skim the books to decide which ones will work best for your particular group and the current ages of the boys. While some of the books on the list for older kids might be okay for your group, some of the lower level books may also work well for an issue that an older group is grappling with. These

suggestions are flexible – a jumping off point to get the dialogue started. I included issues that I strongly feel we must address, but the topics all overlap from one chapter to the next, since they share the same underlying themes.

QUESTIONS FOR HOOT:

- After Roy punches Dana in the face, he tells his dad, "... he was strangling me. What else could I do?" What would you have done in that situation?
- Describe the differences in how the men in the story react to bad news: Curly, Roy's dad, Officer Delinko, Chuck Muckle, Dana's father. Which of them has the healthiest reponse? Least healthy?
- Why do you think Roy, who had never really spoken up about much before, decided to step up and do everything he could to help the owls?
- What would you do if you were in Mullet Fingers' situation? Do you think he is making the best of a bad situation and being resourceful, or do you think he is making a big mistake living the way he does?
- Do you think all the kids getting out of school and protesting at the construction site made a difference? Why or why not?
- Have you ever protested-- either officially or spoken up for something you believe in? What happened?

QUESTIONS FOR THE EPIC FAIL OF ARTURO ZAMORA:

- Bren tells Arturo, "That's how we do in Havana! We fight back!" Abuelo also says this in his letters. Do you think "fighting back" is more inherent in some cultures?
- What do you think inspires Arturo to fight back?
- Arturo is nervous to confess his feelings to Carmen. Reading Abuelo's letter gave him courage to tell her. Do you think you could do something like that?
- Vanessa's group, the "Green Teens" research about the Pipo Place project and really know their stuff. Do you think groups like this can really make a difference, especially if it's made up of only kids?
- Wilfrido says "The only thing that keeps you safe is money." What do you think of that?
- What do you think made the biggest difference in the city's final decision?

QUESTIONS FOR SELMA:

- Why do you think the President (LBJ) won't help Martin Luther King Jr. (MLK) fix voting rights for black citizens in the first part of the movie?
- [Because of all your ancestors endured] "You are already prepared" Amelia says to Coretta Scott King. What does that mean?
- When Jimmy Lee Jackson is shot in the

restaurant, who could they have called for help? What does it mean when you cannot call the police for help?

- During the first march across the bridge (Bloody Sunday) were you surprised by what happened? How did TV coverage affect the power of law enforcement?
- Why do you think the white priest who came to be an ally was beaten and killed?
- The President (LBJ) says to the Alabama governor, "I'll be damned if I'm gonna let history put me in the same place as the likes of you." What does he mean?
- MLK had a no-violence policy. Do you think this was effective? Why or why not?
- How did this movie make you feel about personally speaking up & speaking out?

11
Making the World Better

"Kind people are brave people. Brave is not a feeling that you should wait for. It is a decision. It is a decision that compassion is more important than fear, than fitting in, than following the crowd."
–Glennon Doyle

How do we make the world better as parents and role models? Start with yourself, your family, this book and your book club. We can all do simple things and make small changes on a constant basis. Our sons are bound to notice.

"Leave it cleaner than you found it." My dad always made us pick up trash at the picnic area or the campsite. It didn't matter if it had been left by others, we were responsible as the last ones there. And we couldn't leave until we had picked up some trash. Sometimes we'd have to scan for a gum wrapper or tiny piece of clear plastic. It became a challenge, and if the next people to come along had to clean up after us, they were in for an even bigger challenge.

Back at home we did our chores. There's no need to rethink this classic household tradition. Everyone can help out, and responsibilities can be rotated as often as necessary. Kids generally like to feel like they have a role in family stuff, even when they whine – it's good to be a part of something. They can have input, but they're never off the hook. Schedule them weekly and let the kids prioritize their time and when they get them done. And for goodness sake, please make sure you aren't subconsciously assigning chores according to gender.

Vote. If you're too busy (or lazy) to look up the candidates, you're still covered. Just check out a website such as ballotpedia.org (there are numerous others) and plug in your zip code. You'll find summaries of the candidates' voting histories and priorities. Jot down your own personal cheat sheet and head to your local voting precinct.

While you're at it, talk with your kids about why you vote the way you do, and other specific choices you make. Explain to them why you recycle or choose/avoid specific stores/sites to shop.

Have them sort through all their crap (I use that term affectionately yet realistically, having moved -WITH KIDS - 3 times), and donate clothes, books and toys to charity.

Have them plan, plant and maintain their own gardens. The usefulness of this for practical as well as metaphorical purposes goes without saying. While you're growing your own food, consider going vegetarian a few days a week. Start with Meatless Mondays. Our family has been vegetarian since 2009 and it's not as hard as you may believe! We did it specifically to lessen our carbon footprint.

Let them help you fix things around your home. I know it's often easier to do it yourself, but when my kids want to work on what I'm working on I make a point of letting them help, because it's their home too. By allowing them to take ownership, we raise them up, tighten the family bonds, and eventually, ease our own burden in a way that gives them power and confidence in their real ability to accomplish things. Learning to solve problems is a huge part of growing up.

Go to local events that are important to you. Attend shows, go to rallies, listen to people speak. Share your way of connecting with the greater community. When your child gets to join you as you experience and take part in the arts, politics, outreach,...etc - whatever you value enough to give your time to will begin to resonate with him. Later on he may choose similar ways to take part, or different ways. But he is more likely to want to be a part of larger things, when he has already spent time engaged in events with you.

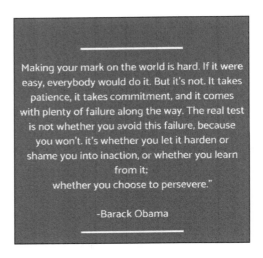

Making your mark on the world is hard. If it were easy, everybody would do it. But it's not. It takes patience, it takes commitment, and it comes with plenty of failure along the way. The real test is not whether you avoid this failure, because you won't. it's whether you let it harden or shame you into inaction, or whether you learn from it; whether you choose to persevere."

-Barack Obama

Healing or repairing the world has long been a general tenet of major philosophies and religions the world over. That includes [healing] the people in it. We only have one planet. We have to share it, and there's no good reason not to take care of one another while we're at it. Kindness, when it's genuine, goes a long, long way. I happen to believe that in many ways, the most valuable lesson to be learned at school, is how to get along with others. It's not something we can Google, or compete in for a winning score or test grade. It can only be practiced - whether in the company of peers or non-peers. We all know adults who have grown-up, but never acquired the skills needed to cooperate and truly accomplish something as a group. As long as we're on the planet, we're in

this group together. We may as well keep practicing.
Maybe our kids can give us some pointers.

DO THIS

Make a list of some simple things you can and WILL do
to break the silence and shake men out of their
mislead masculinity comas. Do it alone, or together
with your son. And, when someone aims a
head-shake or eye-roll at you while mumbling
"women", smile back at him and say firmly "Men."

BOOK RECOMMENDATIONS
on the topic of Making the World Better

3rd graders	~**The 3 Questions** by Jon J. Muth ~The Lorax by Dr. Seuss ~Maniac Magee by Jerry Spinelli
6th graders	~**Operation Redwood** by S. Terrell French ~The Boy Who Harnessed the Wind (novel) by William Kamkwamba and Bryan Mealer ~Be a Changemaker by Laurie Ann Thompson

Movies/ TV	• **Black Panther (2018)** • Zootopia (2016) • The Lorax (2012)

REMINDER:

Pre-read or skim the books to decide which ones will work best for your particular group and the current ages of the boys. While some of the books on the list for older kids might be okay for your group, some of the lower level books may also work well for an issue that an older group is grappling with. These suggestions are flexible – a jumping off point to get the dialogue started. I included issues that I strongly feel we must address, but the topics all overlap from one chapter to the next, since they share the same underlying themes.

QUESTIONS FOR THE THREE QUESTIONS:

- Nikolai seeks help from Leo who has "lived a very long time." Why are the older characters in stories so often the keepers of wisdom? Can young people be wise?
- How would you describe Nikolai? On what do you base your description?
- What does it mean to you to "Live in the moment"?
- How often do you ask your friends for advice? Do they give good advice?
- Can you do good for the person who is beside you if you don't know them? How?

Questions for Operation Redwood:

- Do Julian's aunt & uncle take care of him well? Why or what not?
- Is Danny a good friend? What does he do to try to help Julian?
- Do you think the plan Robin, Danny, and Julian create is smart? Why or why not?
- When Julian becomes friends with Robin, sees her home and land, and learns more about the Redwoods-- does it change his perspective?
- Why do you think Julian is passionate about saving the Redwoods?
- Popo says, "It's good to be enterprising and adventurous", what does that mean?
- Once he is back at Huckleberry Ranch with Danny, they really start working together to save the redwoods. What are the different ideas they come up with and why do you think they succeed?
- Julian and his friends failed a few times trying to carry out Operation Redwood. Did you think they would fail in the end? Why or why not?
- Did reading this book give you good (and not so good) ideas of how to change things you see as unfair?

- T'Challa's father tells him, "You are a good man with a good heart, but it's hard for a good man to be king." What do you think he means by that?
- Nakia says, "I would make a great queen because I'm stubborn." Do you agree?
- Okoye comments, "Guns. So primitive." Imagine for a minute you are from Wakanda-- what would your perspective be of the rest of the world?
- N'Jobu (T'Challa's uncle) tried to fix problems in a different way- which included betrayal- is that sometimes the only way? What did you think of his choices?
- Okoye says to Nakia, "I am loyal to that throne no matter who sits upon it.", but when she is asked (along with other warriors) to kill T'Challa, she makes a different choice. Why do you think she does this?
- Describe the differences between how T'Challa treats women and how Erik (his long-lost cousin) treats women.
- T'Challa addresses the United Nations and says, "The wise build bridges while the foolish build barriers. We must find a way to look after one another as if we are one single tribe." Listening to that speech, do you think he will make the world better? Why or why not? (This comes after the credits roll.)
- Nakia tells T'Challa, "You get to decide what kind of king you are going to be." In the end, what kind of king does he choose to be?

Moving Forward

"...the challenge for parents of sons...is not just to shield their sons from harm; it is to raise sons who will not mistreat girls and women--or remain silent when their peers do."
– Jackson Katz

I could have spent two more years writing and researching for this book. I'm putting it out into the world before it's ready- it's too important, too urgent to wait. My plan is to write a second edition in the next few years with more updated research and statistics, more book and movie recommendations, and hopefully, input from seasoned Father-Son Book Club members (and I can only assume- some corrections!).

While being there for your children is optimal, sometimes you actually need to talk to them. Listen, find out what they're thinking and let them know what you're thinking.

Let's work together to empower our sons against ignorance, prejudice and hatred (anger, sadness, depression, indifference,...etc.).

Here in your hand you have a tangible 10 year (yes! ...ages 8-18) action plan to help your son be the kind of human being who is truly aware of the world around him. He can be aware of the perspectives of others, and strive to do his part to make the world a little bit better.

Please tag me, write to me, send me a telegram, whatever-- tell me about your book club. I'd love to hear what you're doing with the book.

I'm convinced there's at least one boy out there who will turn a corner in his life, and rejoice in all the possibilities of being true to himself, because of a book club. Maybe more...

Dads, caregivers, put your heart into this. Our children are counting on us to act.

"Never forget how important you are to these boys."
–Rosalind Wiseman

Acknowledgements

Lori Day – for writing the book that inspired the book club that inspired this book.

Stacy, Marianne, and my wife Emily – for sharing their book club secrets.

All the people doing the important work out there to help redefine masculinity and encourage and inspire renewed support for boys on their journeys (many of whom are listed in the resources pages) – for your research, your expertise and your heartfelt concern for us as a society that informed and inspired me to write a book worthy of those I hope to serve.

All the baristas at my local Whole Foods coffee bar (especially Randall) – for keeping me caffeinated so I could write this while my kids were asleep.

All my past students, from kindergarten through university – for teaching me through their own authenticity that people of all ages, genders, and self-styled labels have the right to be themselves.

Kevin Barron – for offering his time, perspective, and insight in a way that allowed me to see my own mission more clearly.

My wife, Emily (who is exceptional, and if not for her, this book wouldn't exist) - for her unfailing diligence, her champion resourcefulness, and her thorough collaboration on this book. Her digging, reading, editing, and feedback helped make this book what it is. On top of that, her organization and efficiency kept my nose to the grindstone. She has been equal parts shining light and unrelenting drill sergeant in keeping me focused to get this book out.

My kids- for inspiring me to better the world for them and to help prepare them for the world. After having two girls who were as different as night and day, we foolishly assumed we'd have all girls... but having a son, who was different still, has taught us so much-- most importantly, that all kids are different because of who they are, not because of their gender.

And thank... You - for buying this book and embarking on this collective journey.

Resources

If the resource is mentioned in more than one chapter, it will be listed in the first chapter it is cited.

Introduction

- Day, Lori with Charlotte Kugler. *Her Next Chapter.* Chicago: Chicago Review Press, Incorporated, 2014.
- Fortune, Carley. "Jane The Virgin Star Justin Baldoni Is Exhausted Trying To Be Man Enough". *Flare*, Dec 2017.
- Time's Up Movement, timesupnow.com
- #MeToo Movement, metoomvmt.org
- Black, Michael Ian. "The Boys Are Not Alright". *New York Times*, Feb 2018.
- "Let's Generalize About Men" music video from the show *Crazy Ex-Girlfriend*, 2017.
- Tubin, Hillary. "Reading Role Models: Why They Matter for Boys". Fractuslearning.com, *n.d.*
- Eliot, Lise. *Pink Brain, Blue Brain.* New York: Houghton Mifflin Publishing Company, 2009.
- Orenstein, Peggy. *Cinderella Ate My Daughter.* New York: HarperCollins Publishers, 2011.
- Luscombe, Belinda. "Kids Believe Gender Stereotypes by Age 10, Study Finds". *Time Health*, 2017.
- Katz, Jackson. *The Macho Paradox.* Naperville, IL: Sourcebooks, Inc., 2006.

Chapter 1

- *Late Night With Seth Meyers*, 4/12/2018. Season 5, Episode 91, Guest Jason Reynolds.
- www.Commonsensemedia.org
- www.Goodreads.com

Chapter 2

- Winton, Tim. "About the boys: Tim Winton on how toxic masculinity is shackling men to misogyny". *The Guardian,* April 2018.
- Perry, Grayson. *The Descent of Man.* New York: Penguin Random House LLC, 2016.
- Boddie, Maya J. "The Feminist on Cellblock Y': This Prison Program Elicits Men To Study Feminism, Question Toxic Masculinity" blavity.com, 2018.
- Bennett, Jessica. "A Master's Degree in... Masculinity?" *The New York Times,* August 2015.

Chapter 3

- DeSteno, David. "We're Teaching Grit the Wrong Way". *Chronicle.com,* March 2018.
- Rivera, Diana. Let the Child Cry: How Tears Support Social and Emotional Development". Edutopia.com, Oct 2015.
- Reiner, Andrew. "Talking to Boys the Way We Talk to Girls". *The New York Times,* June 2017.
- Pop Culture Detective. "The Case Against the Jedi Order" YouTube, Dec 2017.
- Burt, Kayti. "Toxic Masculinity is the True Villain of Star Wars: The Last Jedi". Denofgeek.com, May 2018.
- McRobbie, Linda Rodriguez. "The Straight Parents' Guide to How Not to Raise a Homophobe- and How to Be a Better Ally". Slate.com, May 2015.

Chapter 4

- Spence, Blake. "Expanding Masculinity: Moving Beyond Boys Will Be Boys", TedxTalks, Aug 2015.
- Coulson, Dr. Justin. "Boys & Respectful Relationships". South Australia Dept. of Education, Nov 2016.
- Everett, Lucinda. "Morbid? No- Coco is the latest children's film with a crucial life lesson". *TheGuardian.com,* Jan 2018.

Chapter 5

- Bhattacharjee, Yudhijit. "The Science of Good and Evil". *National Geographic*, January 2018.
- Chiaet, Julianne. Chiaet. "Novel Finding: Reading Literary Fiction Improves Empathy". Scientific American, October 2013.
- Eddo-Lodge, Reni. "Why I'm no longer talking to white people about race". Renieddolodge.co.uk, Feb 2014.
- Coates, Ta-Nehisi. Between the World and Me. New York: Spiegel & Grau, 2015.
- Ross, Tracee Ellis. "A woman's fury holds lifetimes of wisdom". TED, April 2018.
- Wiseman, Rosalind. *Masterminds and Wingmen.* New York: Harmony Books, 2013.

Chapter 6

- Gonzalez, Ricardo. "The Impact and Importance of Positive Student-Teacher Relationships". *ELTcenters.com*, July 2016.

Chapter 7

- Samaran, Nora. "The Opposite of Rape Culture is Nurturance Culture". Norasamaran.com, Feb 2016.
- RAINN.org. "What Consent Looks Like". RAINN: Rape, Abuse, and Incest National Network). n.d.
- Murphy, Heather. "What Experts Know About Men Who Rape. *The New York Times*, Oct 2017.
- Chu, Arthur. "Your Princess is in Another Castle: Misogyny, Entitlement, and Nerds." *The Daily Beast*, May 2014.
- MacLaughlin, Kristin. "The Detrimental Effects of Pornography on Small Children." NetNanny.com, Dec 2017.

- *N.a.* "Joseph Gordon Levitt Shares His Thoughts on Porn." Fightthenewdrug.org, Dec 2016.

Chapter 8

- Dawson, James (now Juno). *This Book is Gay.* Naperville, IL: Sourcebooks, Inc, 2015.
- Human Rights Campaign Report. "Growing Up LGBT In America". Hrc.org, 2012
- *The Ellen Show*, 3/1/2018. Season 15, Episode 113, Guest Adam Rippon.
- Davis, Wade. "The Mask of Masculinity". TEDxUF, April 2016.
- Hudson, Matt. "Ex-football player tells story of fitting in, coming out". *Billingsgazette.com*, Jan. 2016.
- LGBTQ Children & Families Resources, pta.org, n.d.
- Johnson, Angela. "7 Ways to Teach Your Kids to Be LGBT Allies". *Romper.com*, June 2016.

Chapter 9

- Wood, Adrian H. "Ten Reasons Middle Schoolers Don't Need Social Media". *Today.com*, Feb. 2018.
- Wakefield, Jane. "Children spend six hours a day or more on screens." BBC News, March 2015.
- Sifferlin, Alexandra. "Here's What Sexist Video Games Do to Boys' Brains". Time.com, April 2016.
- Twenge, Jean M. "Have Smartphones Destroyed a Generation?". *The Atlantic*, Sept 2017.
- Lynch, Matthew. "5 Ways to Teach Digital Citizenship to Your Students"., *thetechadvocate.org*, Jan. 2017.
- *Armchair Expert (Podcast)*, 2/14/2018. Episode 2, Guest Kristen Bell.
- Wait Until 8th Pledge, waituntil8th.org
- Baker, Peter C., "Hunting the Manosphere". *The New York Times*, June 2017.
- Dunckley, Victoria L, M.D. "Why Social Media is Not Smart for Middle School Kids". *Psychology Today*, March 2017.

- Stafford, Rachel Macy. "Tether Yourself: The Enlightening Talk Parents Aren't Having Can Keep Teens from a Damaging Drift." handsfreemama.com, July 2015.

Chapter 10

- Uyehara, Mari. "The Sliming of David Hogg and Emma Gonzalez." *GQ*, March 2018.
- *Davis, Kathleen.* "The Parkland Teens Are Part Of A Long Line Of Kids Who Led Social Change." *Fast Company.com*, Feb 2018.
- Borba, Dr. Michele. "How to Raise Assertive Kids Who Speak Up For Themselves and Others." micheleborba.com, n.d.

Chapter 11

- Doyle, Glennon. "Just Be Kind and Brave". *Momastery.com*, April 2013.
- Ballotpedia.org

A dad of three, Seth Carpenter is a writer, actor, and teacher. He has taught in classrooms and on stages from kindergarten through college since 1995. He has lead workshops and performed with his wife as a character clown for Cirque du Soleil for international audiences. He has traveled extensively, worked as a school teacher, been employed by a law firm, served as a presenter for the Carnegie Museums, taught at four different universities, and served in the U.S. Military. While living in Germany and South Korea, Seth expanded his language skills, increased his cultural awareness, and broadened his perspective on human interaction. In addition to a Masters Degree -including Foreign Language Pedagogy- Seth has trained with The Second City and TheatreSports. He draws upon all of this education and these experiences heavily for inspiration as a father, actor, writer, and speaker. Seth lives in Florida with his wife and kids and not nearly enough toilets for all five of them. His last book was *Haikus of Fatherhood*.

@fathersonbookclubs

Follow @connectwithseth

www.fathersonbookclubs.com

Made in the USA
Middletown, DE
23 February 2019